South Pennine Country

South Pennine Country

by

ROGER A. REDFERN

Photographs by E. Hector Kyme
and the author

ROBERT HALE · LONDON

© *Roger A. Redfern 1979*
First published in Great Britain 1979

ISBN 0 7091 7760 7

Robert Hale Limited
Clerkenwell House
Clerkenwell Green
London EC1R 0HT

Photoset, printed and bound
in Great Britain by
REDWOOD BURN LIMITED
Trowbridge & Esher

Contents

Acknowledgements

It is not possible to mention by name all those who have helped me with the verification of some of the anecdotes herein, but for all their help I thank them.

My thanks go to Mrs W. Craig for the painstaking care she has taken in correcting and typing the manuscript and helping to prepare the index. To my friend E. Hector Kyme I am greatly indebted for providing nine of the photographs used herein.

Illustrations

In the quarry at Little Matlock about 1902

Between pages 144 and 145

The late L. S. Lowry's studio, 'The Elms', Stalybridge Road, Mottram-in-Longdendale

Looking north from the summit of Hollingworthhall Moor on an autumn afternoon

St Chad's church, Saddleworth, in the winter of 1947

Fire at Bankfield Mill, Dobcross, Saddleworth, in January 1947

The south portal of Standedge Tunnel, Huddersfield Narrow Canal, at Diggle

Bosley Locks on the Macclesfield Canal

Hooleyhey Farm beside Lamaload Reservoir, upper Dean Valley.

Kerridge Hill and White Nancy from Ginclough, above Rainow

Adlington Hall beside the River Dean

Red deer in Lyme Park

St Christopher's parish church, Pott Shrigley

The chimney of Danebower Colliery in the upper Dane Valley

The former Eagle and Child Inn at Burntcliff Top, looking towards Allgreave above the Dane Valley

The remains of Gradbach silk mill

The former Keeper's Cottage beside the Barlow Brook at Lee Bridge

The path to the Bull Field, Monk Wood, 1925

Mary and Reuben Dearden at the Pig Gate, Monk Wood, 1920

MAPS

Picture credits

E. Hector Kyme: 5, 6, 10, 19, 28, 37, 38, 44, 45
The author: all other photographs and drawings

1

South Pennine Country

Stand upon Coombes Edge above Longdendale on a bright winter's day and, looking towards the north and north-west, you will see these western fringes of the south Pennines as true escarpment country. Every eminence and every declivity proclaims this region the edge of a huge anticline or upfold, long ago eroded into the delightful variety of hill shapes and valley forms.

Stand upon the top of Puddingpie Hill, four and a half miles west of Chesterfield, and look all about you, again preferably when snow mantles the hills, and you will see more escarpment country, this time a sort of reversed image of that seen on the western side of the main Pennine watershed. An even clearer picture is revealed from the highest point of Fanshawe Gate Lane, near Holmesfield. Looking towards the north, preferably on a June evening, we see an idealized escarpment rising immediately to the west of Totley Hall. Steeply below us, at a much reduced distance, is the scarp slope of the escarpment upon which we stand. It is a rough, gorsy bank far too steep for cultivation. This is the very place where the coal-measures end and the older shales emerge at the foot of the slope, to extend to the place where the heather moors begin on millstone grit, less than a mile to the west of our viewpoint. With the low-angled sun casting good shadows, on a good evening all this escarpment country lies clearly all around us, like the open pages of some wonderful textbook. Here on the eastern flanks of the south Pennines there are scarp and dip slopes, tilted gently eastwards. Here is more evidence – generally clearer to see and understand than on the western side – of the original monster anticline which formed the watershed of the Pennines between the Cheviots and the upper reaches of the Trent Valley.

From the Aire and Ribble valleys in the north, near the place where the carboniferous limestone of the mid-Pennines reaches the surface, to the upper Vale of Trent in the south (a distance of some seventy miles), the true southern Pennines extend as a tract of upland with so much variety and so many stories to tell that one book might do little more than scratch the surface. The width of the region varies greatly but is, at its widest, about thirty-five miles between east and west. The northern part is hemmed between the Lancashire and West Yorkshire textile industrial districts, parts of which climb the slopes and are logically part of these hills. Farther south the uplands reach to the edge of the Cheshire Plain and the industrial lowlands of the Derbyshire coalfield.

Instead of simply scratching the surface of most of the south Pennines, I have attempted to be selective, to go deeper here and there, and so hope to give the reader an impression of life and scenery in that particular place. The traveller here, as anywhere else, cannot hope to know a place and become tainted by its particular character unless he uses his legs and walks. There is nothing more pathetic to me than the traveller who never leaves the highway, the one who glimpses casually some valley or hilly view but never gets to grips with that country.

A large part of the south Pennines lie within the boundaries of the Peak District National Park, but such a frontier should not affect our explorations – there are many fine parts of the region lying outside this National Park, all the better because they are rarely visited: quiet paradises far from roads, car-parks and scenic viewpoints; unassuming country thick still with the associations of working natives and their interesting life-styles, so far removed from the drab lives of modern suburbia not many miles distant as to make the two as different as those of a Bolivian tin-miner and a Norwegian fjord-farmer.

The risk I am taking is that by writing about some of the glorious countryside of this part of upland England I will make it popular and so assist in the destruction of its particular magic. Knowing that relatively few will bother to use time and energy to go there, I think I am on safe ground.

2

Yesterday But A Dream –
The Drone Valley

One mile north of Chesterfield's famous crooked spire in north Derbyshire lies the rather drab industrial-cum-residential sprawl called Whittington Moor. It is here, well out of sight, close beside a railway embankment, that the meandering River Rother is joined by a small stream that has wound down, in a generally south-easterly direction, for some seven miles through a valley that it is easy to underestimate in terms of historical importance and natural beauty. The stream is the River Drone, and its sinuous vale is that followed by the Derby-Leeds trunk-road (A61). The recent construction of a by-pass has reduced the traffic through the valley.

The major settlement is the ancient market town of Dronfield, which lies near the head of the vale. Its original, rustic character was largely changed by the coming of industrialization and, in the last quarter-century, by large-scale residential expansion by over-spill from nearby Sheffield.

The Drone begins life as a spring at seven hundred feet, close to the Derbyshire-South Yorkshire border near Mickley, and flows eastwards, then southwards into the main alignment of its valley. Here stands central Dronfield, containing the church of St John the Baptist (largely early-fourteenth century), the ancient cruck barn thought to have been the original *aula* (dwelling) of the sixth-century Anglian chieftain, and the early-eighteenth-century Manor House commanding the head of the High Street. This is the old heart of the town, but industrialization developed in the valley-bottom close to the river.

There was much small-scale coal-mining in the Drone Valley, nowhere more intensely than in the Hill Top district to the

11

south of Dronfield. Over the watershed to the north and north-east, tool-making developed into an important industry – little villages such as Ridgeway and Eckington became notable for the quality of their edge-tools, particularly scythes and sickles. Such an early reputation did not attach to Dronfield; there is no evidence of this early tool trade here, and the reason is not known today.

However, in and about the town are many fairly large stone houses that date mainly from the seventeenth century. Such dwellings include Chiverton House, Rose Hill and The Cottage. The late W. N. Dixon pointed out that many lead merchants lived in the little township in former times, perhaps because it was a more desirable locality than Chesterfield, a known centre of the Derbyshire lead trade. Some of these fine houses probably owe their very existence to such wealthy tradesmen.

Close beside the Drone, where it flows at the foot of Dronfield's parish churchyard, was established in 1790 what is reputedly the first foundry to produce malleable iron castings. Samuel Lucas opened his works here and patented the process for the castings of malleable iron in 1804. This works, later called Edward Lucas and Son Ltd, was known locally as 'the Bottom Yard' to differentiate it from another Lucas works two hundred yards upstream that used a tilt hammer (hence the local designation 'the Tilt'). On Christmas Eve 1971 the last castings were produced at 'the Bottom Yard', and subsequently the works was demolished. Only the archway that was the original entrance to the foundry remains, centrepiece of a pleasant garden beside the London-Leeds railway route through the valley.

It was the lack of a convenient railway link that delayed the industrial development of Dronfield. George Stephenson chose the neighbouring Rother Valley to take his main line between Derby and Leeds because it offered fewer physical problems. Finally, in 1870 the line up the Drone Valley was opened, and this placed Sheffield on a major route to the south. With the coming of the railway, Dronfield assumed the role of an industrial town, pushing the countryside back a little.

That delightful, steep-sided country of patchwork fields punctuated with a dozen woods is still there to be explored; the field paths are there, and the vistas are waiting at every bend, from the hill-tops to the intricacies of wooded river-sides.

The river flows southwards towards the Rother, hemmed in by high ground attaining the seven-hundred-foot contour to both east and west. High upon the eastern heights stand the settlements of Summerley, Apperknowle and Hundall. An ancient bridle-track goes up from Dronfield to Summerley, a tiny place with a couple of farms, a Hall and several cottages. The name means 'summer pasture' and is more likely to have served as such for the valley-bottom village of Unstone than for Dronfield.

Summerley Hall was probably built about 1300, when Unstone Manor was divided between two daughters of the owner of the estate. The present house is the result of a major rebuilding after 1650 and is typical of several yeoman halls of the district built about the same time. The Curtiss family lived here for a long period. Francis Curtiss went to school at Southwell, Nottinghamshire, and later to Cambridge, in the seventeenth century. Thomas Curtiss was a master at Dronfield's Henry Fanshawe School, and, being last of the line, the property was sold after his death in 1701.

Half a mile along the lane to the south-east lies the larger village of Apperknowle – 'apple tree hill' – which grew during the last century with the discovery of productive coal seams close to the surface here. Coal was sent down a cable-hauled railway to the main line at Unstone, and the course of this steep route can still be made out when a low sun etches the cuttings with telltale shadow. A further half-mile to the south-east lies Hundall, a hill-crest hamlet taking its name from a combination of terms that mean 'dogs' hill'.

Near the place where the steep lanes from Apperknowle and Hundall meet, down near the valley floor, stands the village of Unstone. Like Apperknowle, the countenance of this settlement was much modified by coal-mining during the nineteenth century, though now most of the scars are hidden.

Mrs K. Battye, who has done considerable research into the history of this village, points out that in Saxon times Unstone was held by Lewin and Edwin, sons of Leofric, King of Mercia. After the Norman Conquest it was granted to the Brailsfords; subsequently the estate passed through several families and in the fifteenth century came to the Bullocks. During the Civil War the Bullocks fell on hard times, but not so hard as to prevent the rebuilding of Unstone Manor in about 1653. This is an L-shaped gabled manor house typical of many that survive throughout north Derbyshire.

Immediately downstream of Unstone the hillsides hem the river in, forming a wooded gorge. Here stood one of the village's two water-mills; the attractive Mill House is still occupied, all but engulfed by tall trees by the quiet Drone. Close by, the busy railway strides across the dale on its high, masonry viaduct, the most impressive feature on the journey between Chesterfield and Sheffield.

From the steep hill path leading south-westwards from Unstone Manor to the Hill Top district of Dronfield there are broad views back to Apperknowle and across the narrowing confines of the gorge at Unstone to Glasshouse Hill (664 feet), the most conspicuous eminence of the district. Grasscroft Wood clothes its crest on the southern side, emphasizing its shape and casting mysterious shadows at a summer sundown.

Downstream of the Unstone gorge the little river, often ochre-tinged from the disused colliery drains, meanders on beneath Brierley Bridge to Sheepbridge. Here it is joined by the Barlow Brook – its major tributary – and flows grey and rubbish-strewn by engineering works and railway sidings, to be swallowed unceremoniously by the Rother at Whittington Moor.

Among the inhabitants who peopled this river hollow there were many memorable characters, complete individuals in their own right who have not been replaced. To each generation of perceptive children there were folk about who amused or intrigued or terrified – the simple-minded, the aged, the crippled and the recluse. There were nicknames as apt as they were useful for differentiation: Jobber, the Rat, Mucky Barker, Monkey Face and Vinegar Face, Tiptoe, Sonnie and Laughing Hyena.

Areas of Dronfield – rows of houses, even single dwellings – had nicknames too. Spring Gardens (now part of Lea Road) has a tall terrace always referred to as 'Curtain Row' because the occupants vied with one another on the matter of the best lace curtains. 'Mud Row', Scarsdale Road, was built by my great-grandfather William ('Cakey') Ward Barker and had outside walls covered with concrete to keep them dry. 'Whisky Bank', Unstone, got its name because certain occupants were noted for their predilection for that beverage, while 'Heavenly Row', Cross Lane, has long since gone but is remembered for its pointed, gothic-style windows.

Up near the source of the River Drone lived, during my childhood, and for many years before and after, a character known to everyone as Len. His real name is Len Organ, and his stiff, stumping gait was known to all the inhabitants of Stubley Lane and Dronfield Woodhouse for more than thirty years up to 1965. He originated in Manchester and emigrated in his teens to New South Wales, Australia, where he was a boundary-rider on a cattle station. At the outbreak of World War I he was twenty-one and volunteered for the Australian Army. In the Dardanelles he suffered severe frost-bite and lost all his toes, so coming back to this country and working thereafter on farms in north Derbyshire. When we knew him, he was living in an old tent beside the headwaters of the Drone, not far from the place where Barnes Lane crossed it between Barnes Farm and Upper Birchitt Farm. I recall a summer day when we came up beside the stream from the spot where it crosses the railway cutting on an aqueduct near Bradway Tunnel. There was no one about – Len was not at home. With a feeling compounded of fascination and terror we peered inside the hovel and saw, to our surprise, a huge pile of books. Why all those books?

Down the bank beside the stream we found the place where Len hewed his coal from an outcropping seam, a thing he did for many years until infirmity prevented it and then he bought fuel. He must have been working on the farm that day for we never caught sight of him; but we went away wondering about all those books. Some time later the *Derbyshire Times* reported the case of several hundred books having disappeared from Dronfield County Library and being found in Len's hut beside the Drone. He explained that he was a keen reader and in order to borrow more books than was his due he always brought out from the library a few extra underneath his raincoat. When discovered, a lot of the books had been ruined by damp and the remainder were sent away to be fumigated. Len promised never again to take away more than his fair share of books – and he never did.

Between 1953 and 1965 he lived in a wooden hut he fabri-
cated from odd timber and old fertilizer bags, beside the same
stream.

"Nobody wanted a useless old man like me, so I took to living
like this," he said to a newspaper reporter in November 1965. It
was then that he finally decided, at the age of seventy-two, to
give up the outdoor life and went to Newholme Hospital, Bakewell. "In a home I shall be warmer this winter and won't have
to bother about where the next meal is coming from; but in
summer, then I shall miss living here," he said with a sadness
natural after a virtual lifetime in the open air. In those later
years beside the Drone, Len spent his days watching the natural world and farmers at work where he, too, had once worked
vigorously.

But Len was never a recluse in the true sense of the word for
there was nothing he liked better than to hold forth on topics of
world importance in the tap room of the old inn at Stubley, to
which he made his way on several evenings each week. Len
Organ still (1978) lives at Newholme Hospital and is in good
health, though he now rarely goes outside.

Mention of Stubley recalls the fact that there was once a row
of stone cottages on the south side of Stubley Hollow, not far
below its junction with Stubley Lane. They were dark places,
down in the shadow of tall, overhanging trees, and they looked
towards the north. To children of an earlier generation the top
of Stubley Hollow was the very gate of Hell; and the dirty old
woman who dwelt in one of these gloomy houses terrified young
passers-by. To them 'Annie-O', as she was generally known,
conveyed a sort of fascinating horror similar to that engendered
in us thirty years later by the ancient, crook-fingered Mrs Sykes
of the Red Lion Inn. Annie-O sported a wide-brimmed, black
hat in all seasons, beneath it her sooty face looked out at the
world. On her arm was a wicker basket into which were placed
all the odds and ends she found in gutter and hedgerow. There
seems to have been an unreliable water supply to those dark
cottages in Stubley Hollow, and that, no doubt, accounted in
part for the old girl's grubby countenance, though poverty was
not unknown to a good many Dronfield people in those days,
and that often brought apathy in its wake.

There were many characters at the heart of old Dronfield, too. At the close of the thirties, the High Street end of Farwater Lane had dwellings on both sides, but all those on the east side, including the beautiful Elizabethan Masons' Arms Inn, had been empty some years. Those on the west side were still occupied, as was the tree-dotted area behind called Eldon Croft. According to an unpublished survey of 1561, this area was known as Elton Croft, possibly after a family originating from Elton, near Winster, but that is only a conjecture. Whatever the origin of the name, Eldon Croft was a grand place, and with some imagination the local council could have made this a most desirable part of the old town. Instead its inhabitants were moved to new housing, and the old properties fell into decay; finally the area was cleared and grass, nettles and willowherb took over.

On the sloping ground below the site of Eldon Croft in those later years lupins blossomed among the tall grass, a reminder of the days when there were allotment gardens overlooking Farwater Lane. I remember going each spring to a cottage in the Croft to ask for Mr Dent and being taken down by him, an old man by that time, to his green garden. He carried a newspaper and string with him, and when he reached the allotment a trowel would be produced from a shed – there was a collection of old buildings, a greenhouse, potting shed, cold frames, all well patched with tarred felt and wood and showing their age. We would walk on down to the brassica crop and there Mr Dent carefully lifted the young cabbages and Brussels sprouts, wrapped them in the newspaper and tied the bundles with string. Then I would pay him what I remember being a ludicrously small amount – a shilling or two – and he would set me off up the path, saying "I've got a few jobs to do before I come up, lad," and I would return up the slope, through Eldon Croft and across the top of Farwater Lane to home.

Those blue lupins in the waving grass were memorials to Mr Dent and the rest of the inhabitants of Eldon Croft. They have now been swept away and replaced by the ugly, barren tarmac, bricks and concrete of the Civic Centre.

Immediately after World War II there came down Dronfield's High Street on most evenings a pair of funny characters, out for a good time in one or other of the hostelries in that part of town. They were Comic Grindlow (alias Taylor) and his sister. It was said that Comic had suffered shell-shock in the Great War and never been the same again; whatever it was, he certainly acted strangely. His appearance was tattered to say the least, and it seemed to get more ragged as he got older; to make this worse he went for days – even weeks, it seemed – without a shave. The sister was a tiny, mouse-like creature with the palid complexion of a church mouse. It was said that their cottage in Stubley Hollow contained but one bed, and so they took turns to sleep in it. Comic slept at night, she during the day, hence the pale face. During the evening, though, brother and sister were up and about; this was the time for their expedition to the town centre.

Watching from the top of the old wall which surrounded our garden or from the monument in the middle of the street, I would see Comic appear round the corner near Manor Farm. By the time he had got twenty yards down the street, the tiny sister would come into view, trotting to maintain a constant distance behind him. The old chap always wore a pair of down-at-heel boots, often unlaced, and had the habit of kicking one heel with the other toe; this led to a somewhat halting progress down High Street – a few steps, a hesitation while he kicked at one or other heel, then on again. The next manœuvre was also habitual. As soon as he drew opposite the door of the Blue Stoops Inn, he looked about him and when the scurrying sister had almost caught up, he said "I'll just look inside to see if he's there." With that he crossed the street and disappeared from sight inside The Blue Stoops. Seconds later his face appeared at the open door as he beckoned to her, shouting so that any passers-by could hear, "Yes, he's in – come in a minute." With that they both entered the noise and the smoky atmosphere, where they often stayed until closing time. The Grindlows must have had a guilty feeling about going into public houses, and by adopting this approach they apparently felt that honour had been saved, simply going in to see an acquaintance who did not, in fact, exist.

3

The Gosforth Valley

This broad, shallow valley stretches westwards for more than a mile from the old centre of Dronfield in north-east Derbyshire. It now contains what is claimed to be the largest private housing development in the country.

The great majority of people now living in the valley never knew the area before it became inundated by bricks, concrete and tarmac, starting in 1965.

Measured on the map it is one and a quarter miles from the Manor House (now Dronfield's Public Library) to the top of the little ridge south of Dronfield Woodhouse which marks the western limit of the valley. From Stubley (on the B6056 road) southwards across the width of the valley to the top of the ridge adjoining Cowley Lane it is almost three quarters of a mile.

For such an extensive bowl or shallow vale the stream which drains it is surprisingly small. It is generally called the Gosforth Brook and for much of its course runs underground. Only in its lower course – called the Lea Brook – did the stream ever run regularly upon the surface, and then only in winter and wet, summer weather. This stream runs below Fanshawe Bank, beneath the former Congregational Chapel adjoining Lea Road, and then joins the parent River Drone beside the site of Dronfield Railway Station.

Down at this confluence it is about 450 feet above sea level, and the crest of the little ridge at the head of the valley lies at 725 feet. These are the two extremes of altitude in the Gosforth Valley. The ridge-top bounding it on the southern side reaches 650 feet between the Hyde Park Inn (at Dronfield Hill Top) and Hills Farm.

It is more accurate to call this lowland a bowl than a valley.

PREHISTORY

During the mid- and late 1950s the figure of Captain Horace Grainger was often to be seen searching the fields of the Gosforth Valley. Captain Grainger became an enthusiastic amateur archæologist and made several interesting discoveries in the Dronfield district, and farther afield in the Peak District.

He recruited small parties of boys to assist in the work of excavation, and though many local people treated his field work with scepticism and amusement he did reveal unusual features beneath the pastoral quiet of the valley.

One of the most interesting things Captain Grainger and his young assistants unearthed was a large and curiously shaped block of rock which he designated a Fertility Stone, a sort of altar which had featured in pre-Christian rites. It stood where it had been excavated, near the stream where it runs beneath the tall trees to the south-west of the Civic Centre. When large drains were constructed before the housing developments commenced, this large stone was set in concrete in the bed of a major drain outfall just to the south of the stream and is still visible though not very obvious.

Some distance westwards upstream, near the place where the old Gosforth Lane crossed the bottom of the valley on a raised causeway (and close to the point where the present Gosforth Lane crosses the valley en route for Hill Top), Captain Grainger exposed a grave beside the stream. He identified a Skull Stone on a shelf with boulders below it on a pavement. The whole structure was about four feet deep. The grave had a drain into the stream.

ROUTEWAYS

The major route of the valley was the lane which left the top of Dronfield High Street beside the Manor Farm and wound westwards, forking in three quarters of a mile. The left fork crossed over the ridge and out of the valley by Woodend Farm, through Kitchen Wood and so to Cowley Lane. The right fork rose more gradually to Dronfield Woodhouse. This right fork and about half the lane between the fork and Dronfield was called Oxclose Lane – an old name which originated prior to

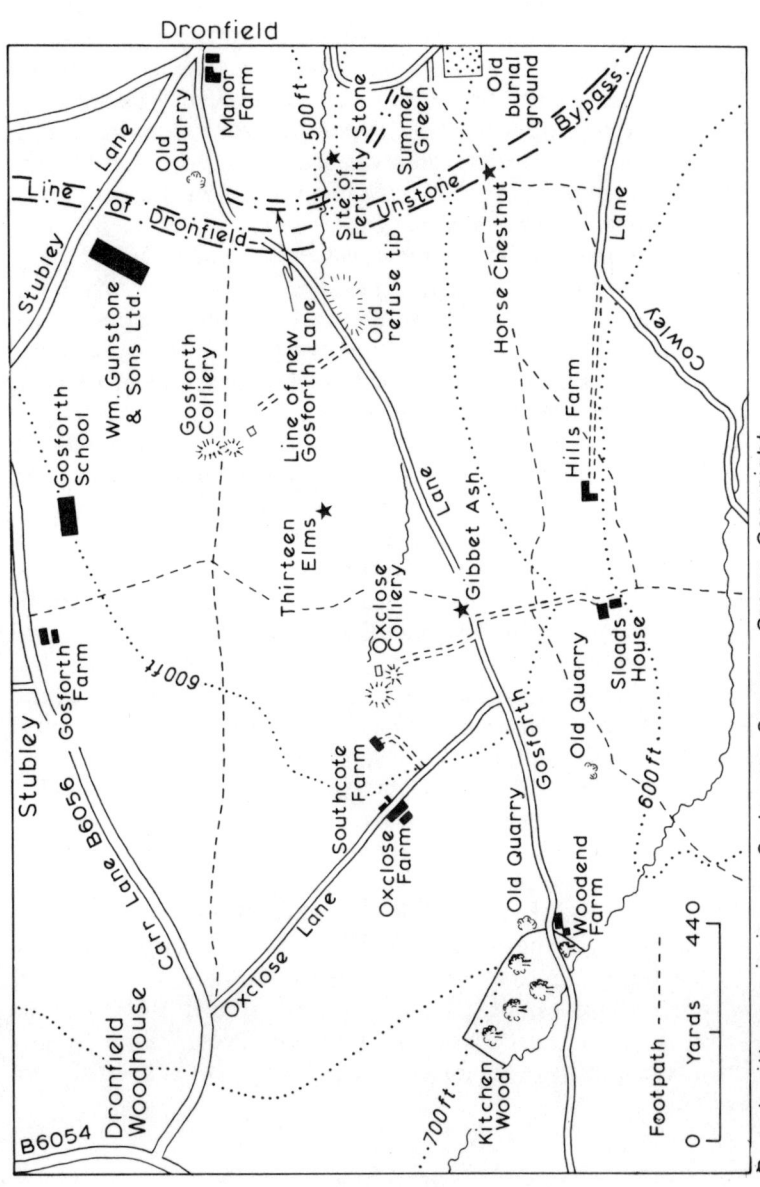

THE GOSFORTH VALLEY BEFORE DEVELOPMENT

Based with permission on Ordnance Survey. Crown Copyright.

the sixteenth century because a survey of 1561 refers to 'Ox cloose'. That part of the lane nearest Dronfield was Gosforth Lane and had been for an equally long time. The name appears to mean 'gorse ford'. Some old maps – a surveyor's preliminary sketch map dating from the first part of the nineteenth century is one such – refer to this routeway as 'Gorseybrigg Lane', from Dronfield right up to the fork. 'Gorseybrigg' means literally 'a gorse-covered bank or slope'.

Most of the footpaths which crossed the valley were of considerable antiquity, originating as direct routes between hamlets (such as Stubley) and Dronfield and outlying farms. One of these paths left Gosforth Lane just west of the last houses and crossed ten fields due westwards to the junction of Oxclose Lane with the B6056 road. It was a much-used route right up to the development of this gentle northern flank of the valley. It was crossed by a pair of paths which joined Stubley to Gosforth Lane.

Another footpath crossed the highest part of the southern flank of the valley, between Summer Green and Hills Farm en route for Cowley. From it in sunny weather the whole of the valley lay in view, a patchwork of fields and scattered woods and hidden farms.

Between the autumns of 1973 and 1975 the lower part of the Gosforth Valley was further despoiled by the construction of the Unstone-Dronfield Bypass, for the A61 (Exeter-Leeds) trunk road. This dual-carriageway sweeps through a broad cutting from the south, down into the valley and high above the new house-tops upon a disastrously ugly viaduct. This concrete construction has earned the local name of 'Stonehenge', something of an insult to the skill and aesthetic sense of our Bronze Age ancestors living on Salisbury Plain.

The headlong roar and atmospheric pollution associated with the by-pass since it was opened to traffic on 16th October 1975, is in such direct contrast with the tree-girt and hedge-hung tranquillity of the former valley routeways as to be almost unbelievable.

FIELD AND WOODLAND NAMES

As so often throughout the British countryside, the field names here tell us something about the past.

In a plan dated 13th March 1876 showing 'Dronfield Grammar School Lands' parts of the first two fields to the north of Gosforth Lane on leaving Dronfield are referred to as the 'Town-field Dole' – literally 'a share or portion of the Town Field' which was one of the large fields of the medieval three-field system. Directly opposite this field, across Gosforth Lane, lay the Gosford Field (3½ acres). This stretched down to the bank of the Lea Brook and was presumably a gorsy slope in former times, where the stream could easily be crossed.

The large, rectangular fields which occupied the southern slopes nearest the former Farwater Lane (now called Gosforth Lane) were called the Finney Fields. In 1524 they were known as 'le Fynnesse', deriving their name from the Old English '*fennig*' – fenny or marsh ground. In the past four centuries their character has certainly changed for they were, in this century, fairly dry and fertile fields. The 1876 plan shows part of the Upper Finney (over two acres) as belonging to Dronfield Grammar School. In a schedule of the Charity Commission dated 21st January 1881, another part of the Finney Fields is shown to have been a portion of the Charity of the Reverend Lawrence Banks. This consisted of "an undivided portion of a field called the Great Finney, containing one acre and nine perches". It is interesting to note that these very fields were the first to be built upon at the commencement of the new developments in 1965.

There were no large woods in the valley. The plantation to the south-west of the Manor House, adjoining Farwater Lane, contains some fine specimen beech trees, and happily most of it remains, albeit as a somewhat artificial 'town park'. Here, on both sides of Lea Brook, a colony of the very rare Autumn Crocus (*Crocus nudiflorus*) has long been established. The nearby development has caused a reduction in the colony, and the blooms are more subject to trampling and plucking in September than they used to be. The colony is well worth preservation, being virtually unique in this part of England.

The more extensive Kitchen Wood lies immediately to the west of the ridge at the upper end of the valley and so does not lie strictly within the compass of this brief study.

Several outstanding trees grew about the vale, some of them still extant though now robbed of their rural dignity by the adjacent desert of bricks and mortar.

The Thirteen Elms occupy a central position in the valley. They are old trees standing in a hedgerow not far from the former footpath between Gosforth Colliery and Dronfield Woodhouse. At the time of writing they remain intact.

Likewise the Gibbet Ash stands beside the former Oxclose Lane, opposite the place where the track to Sloads House joined it. Thirty years ago this large tree had a dead fox hanging by a rope from one of its branches – a warning to others – and its dried remains swung there for a long time. It was a place of mystery and horror to a child's imagination.

High on the Finney Fields rose what was the finest tree in the whole valley. The broad-trunked and beautifully proportioned horse chestnut was the first tree passed on the footpath from Summer Green to Cowley. It was intended to spare the tree when the Unstone-Dronfield Bypass was constructed, but due to bungling of the development plans the cutting containing the new road had to extend farther west than originally intended, and this great specimen was quietly felled in 1973. This represents one of the most disgraceful acts of vandalism by the Philistines responsible for the destruction of the valley and its heritage.

DWELLINGS

The valley was never thickly populated. Few dwellings occupied the main body of this area; fewer of them remain.

At the eastern end of Gosforth Lane stands Manor Farm, adjacent to the Manor House at the top of Dronfield's High Street. The farmhouse is not very old, but the yard and buildings date from a much earlier period. It formed part of the Cecil Estate until recent years, and its more than one hundred acres lay within the lower (eastern) part of the valley. Its old yard is still girt with attractive buildings, and a large flock of muscovy ducks used to dibble in the pond or preen themselves by its edge in view of the kitchen door.

The land falls away to the south of the farm to the bottom of the valley, where ancient Farwater Lane dipped *en route* for Dronfield Hill Top. Down by the Lea Brook stood some delightful cottages, set back from the lane below Moonpenny Farm across productive gardens. They were swept away as being unfit for human habitation, but foresight and common sense could have given them a new lease of life and maintained the charm of the lower valley.

Half a mile to the south-west of the lower Lea Brook and immediately beyond the ridge-top stands Hills Farm. It stands on the very limit of the valley and looks out over the headwaters of the brooks which finally drain southwards into the Barlow Brook near Lee Bridge. Hills Farm was originally a farm worker's smallholding belonging to nearby Shirecliffe Farm. The Timperley family moved here about 1895, and when the son married an extra portion was erected on the eastern end of the farmhouse (about 1906). This newer dwelling is taller than the original house, and here lives the Bingham family. Mr Arnold Bingham is a well-known character, a retired threshing contractor, and his wife is a member of the Timperley family. She was born here at Hills Farm soon after her parents moved there towards the end of the last century.

One field distant to the west lie the remains of ancient Sloads House, known to many people in the district as 'the ghost house' on account of its derelict condition. In a survey undertaken in 1561, the dwelling was referred to as 'the Slades', and in a document of 1649 in the Wheat Collection (now in Sheffield Public Library) 'Slodes Dole' is mentioned. The name is derived from the Old English word *'slaed'* – a valley. Sloads House stands upon a shallow pass on the southern ridge at the edge of the Gosforth Valley, and overlooks the wooded valley country to the south.

The property constituted a small farm belonging to the illustrious Miss Charlotte Ward of Dronfield (who died in March 1971). It required considerable work to bring it up to the local authority's standards for continued habitation. This work was not done, and the last tenants, the Sharpe family, vacated the house prior to World War II. In front of the house was a deep well (though partly filled in, it can still be seen) over which lies an old gravestone. I imagine that it came at some time from the old burial-ground at Summer Green, a useful coverstone for the well-head.

Six hundred yards along the ridge to the west stands Wood-end Farm, a smallholding at the very edge of Kitchen Wood. On large-scale Ordnance Survey maps it is called 'Steward's House'. As often happened when the early OS field-officers covered the ground on foot, obtaining local information to add to the first OS maps, they made mistakes, and here is a good example. One Stewart Black built this dwelling beside Kitchen Wood early in the nineteenth century, and it became known locally as 'Stewart's House' – the field-officer either mis-heard or mis-spelt what he was told! Woodend Farm was one of the first dairy farms in this part of Derbyshire to gain a certificate for tuberculin-free milk. Just prior to World War II the rent for this smallholding was one pound a year more than that for Sloads House.

The lane which comes up through Kitchen Wood from Cowley Lane passes Woodend Farm, crosses the ridge (where there is a broad and once-lovely view eastwards down the Gosforth Valley to the spire of St John's church, Dronfield). A short distance down the slope the lane joined Oxclose Lane, where the latter turned sharply towards Dronfield Woodhouse.

Three hundred yards up the lane stood ancient Oxclose Farm, actually two holdings, their dwellings semi-detached. Some large deciduous trees stood adjacent to the houses and outbuildings here. The setting was most attractive; fowls scratched along the lane, and one could see into the buildings. As often as not, the kitchen door lay open to reveal a blazing fire within. The Elliott family came here in 1925 and left in 1971, when the entire settlement was demolished during October of that year. The Bonser family farmed the other part of Oxclose Farm, occupying the house on the south-east side. Mr C. Bonser remembers that the family took the tenancy here in 1906.

My maternal great-grandfather was William Ward ('Cakey') Barker, who was born at Quoit Green House, Hallowes Lane, Dronfield in 1830 and died there in 1916. His great-great-grandfather was William Ward, who is known to have been farming at Oxclose in 1768.

Across the field to the east of Oxclose Farm stood Southcote Farm. It is a post-1846 development because on an Enclosure

Award map of that date it is not shown. Its pseudo-battlements peering from behind the surrounding trees always fascinated me as a child, lending something of a fairy-tale aspect to this upper reach of the valley. The Bird family farmed at Southcote until the recent developments, since which time it has been modernized as a private dwelling surrounded by tasteless brick houses and busy roads.

The very first housing development in this upper part of the valley was the construction of new dwellings in a cul-de-sac off Oxclose Lane called Oxclose Drive, soon after the Second World War.

The Dronfield district's most celebrated living native lives here. John Dethick believes he is a descendant of the famous Dethicks of Dethick near Matlock. Initially trained as a singer locally, he was advised by Sir Henry Wood to make singing a career and later studied with him in London. He is one of the world's leading bass-baritones and is generally considered the outstanding interpreter of Mendelssohn's *Elijah*, having sung that role more than 150 times in many parts of the world. John Dethick is greatly in demand, and his repertoire ranges from Bach's *St Matthew Passion*, Handel's *Messiah* and Elgar's *Dream of Gerontius* through Fauré and Honegger to Vaughan Williams, Walton and Stanford. He is President of the Sheffield Bach Society and teaches singing most successfully; his pupils are now performing as principals in most of the opera companies in this country.

The oldest building in the Gosforth Valley stands at the northern perimeter, at Stubley. It is the very ancient cruck barn at Gosforth Farm, close behind the modern Stubley Garage. The illustrious Stubley family lived here in the Middle Ages (in 1307 John de Stubbeleye was probably resident here) taking their name from this place, an outlying hamlet with an Old English name meaning literally 'tree stump clearing'. The late Mrs Bessie Bunker suggests in her book *Cruck Buildings* (published 1970) that the cruck barn at Gosforth Farm was originally erected by the Angles as early as the sixth century, as were, she contended, so many of the cruck buildings of North Derbyshire and South Yorkshire. What remains here at Stubley is three sets of oaken crucks – there were probably originally two or three more sets of crucks which could have been removed when the later farmhouse was built. The building would have been wooden walled and roofed with thatch, replaced when stone began to be used widely for building purposes. It is now roofed with asbestos sheets.

INDUSTRY

The carboniferous coal-measures which cover much of the surface of north-east Derbyshire produced fertile soils in the Gosforth Valley. This was typical mixed farming country, notable for high yields of wheat, barley, oats and potatoes.

Beneath the surface these same coal-measures contained coal-seams of considerable importance. Where these seams came close to the surface there was small-scale opencast mining from a comparatively early date, and several old bell pits were exposed when the Unstone-Dronfield Bypass was being constructed across the valley, but the two collieries established here in Victorian times are of greatest interest today.

The site of Oxclose Colliery can still be seen a short distance to the east of Southcote Farm. The extensive waste-tips are now clothed with silver birches and are to be retained as a scenic feature. The earliest record of this colliery dates from 1867. Its abandonment presents something of a mystery for it was, in fact, abandoned twice.

According to the National Coal Board's 'List of Abandoned Mines', it was first closed by Andrews Brothers on 4th November 1882; a second record of abandonment exists and is attributed to E. Knight in December 1882. Was the colliery in fact worked in two parts by separate parties? This would have been most unusual and seems unlikely. Did a small operator called Knight take over from Andrews Brothers in the hope of making something of the abandoned colliery? If so, his independent effort lasted only one month.

The other enterprise was the Gosforth Colliery; it stood half a mile due west of Dronfield's Manor House and three hundred yards south-east of the present Gosforth School (opened 1955). It was approached by a cart-track leading northwards from Gosforth Lane. This important colliery was worked by the Silkstone Colliery Company and was also abandoned in 1882 but was soon afterwards re-opened and operated by John Sheard &

Co, of Gomersal Farm, Dronfield. It proved a successful gamble on the part of this Dronfield landowner and contractor. My great-grandfather's diary entry for Friday 6th October 1893 states: "Fine. Went up to Sheard's pit, never seen such a sight in my life. More than two hundred carts waiting for coal, which is 17/6 per ton for best." Later, on Friday 10th December 1893, we read: "Fine. Been to Bull Close and Sheard's Pit to get load of coals but did not succeed – so many carts waiting." This boom time at Gosforth Colliery continued for nine years more. Mr Sheard had the reputation of being a hard business man. He farmed some of the Finney Fields on the south side of the valley, land crossed daily by those of his miners living at Hill Top. For "damage suffered to the surface of my land" by these miners taking a short cut to the pit, Sheard is reputed to have subtracted a portion of their wages each week.

Finally, in 1902, Gosforth Colliery was abandoned for the last time, partly because the coal was proving difficult to extract and partly through the continued serious flooding of the workings.

The gaunt, brick chimney continued to dominate the lower valley until the mid-fifties, when it was demolished. The winding-house, coke ovens and tip were well concealed by elder, birch and briars, a fascinating sort of place. The two shafts had great interest for generations of boys, who climbed to peer into the void and hear distantly the trickle of subterranean waters. A man who lived in a cottage in Stubley Hollow disappeared one day soon after World War I, and it was always thought that he had fallen down one of these shafts: an unsolved mystery.

The shafts were filled in by the NCB during the fifties, and during 1975 the tip and remaining buildings were removed and houses built upon the site.

At various times through this century opencast mining has taken place in the valley. The occupants of Woodend Farm, for instance, are known to have dug their own coal to the east of the farm during the colliers' strike in the twenties.

During the latter part of the nineteenth century William Prestwich began making iron castings in modest premises adjoining Gosforth Colliery. This was called Gosforth Foundry. Two moulders and a boy made up the workforce. Some time during the nineties Gosforth Foundry moved to new premises at California Works, Mill Lane, Dronfield, and later to Callywhite Lane, where the factory retained the name Gosforth Foundry.

At the western end of Victoria Street, three fields distant from Gosforth Colliery, was the quarry operated by the Bingham family at the beginning of this century. From it was extracted much building stone.

On the south side of Gosforth Lane, near the place where the tract branched to Gosforth Colliery, was the town's one-time refuse-tip. Rubbish started to be piled here about 1900, and Mr C. Bonser of Oxclose Farm recalls the sight of council horses and carts moving along the lane, mounting the side of the tip and dumping rubbish there. When tipping ceased about 1920, soil was brought in cartloads to cover it. Thereafter the steep-sided mound was colonized by elder, willowherb and briars. In early post-war years goats were tethered there to browse on the bushes, and Dronfield folk went there to cut rhubarb and dig horse-radish.

The most recent industrial development occurred on the northern edge of the lower valley, on the site of allotment gardens beside Stubley Lane. Here I remember well the tall figure of Mr Tom Elliott of Cowley, who walked across the valley each day to work in his garden. He rested in his hedge-side hut, puffing at a pipe and surrounded by tools and seed boxes. Messrs William Gunstone & Sons purchased this site and built their new bakery on it, moving from Duke Street, Sheffield and starting production here during November 1951.

A WALK IN MEMORY

Though public rights of way still allow one to walk across parts of the valley, the fascination has all but gone. The delights are left largely in the memory.

The western end of Gomersal Lane joins the former Farwater Lane (now called Gosforth Lane) at what was known evocatively as Summer Green. On a summer day the view across the wooded lower part of the Gosforth Valley revealed the old cluster of buildings about Dronfield's High Street, the spire of St John's church rising to the right, and far away behind the patchwork of hedged fields beyond the Drone Valley Coal

Aston stood upon its hill-top to the north-east.

Across Farwater Lane a footpath went between hawthorn hedges – a sort of passage – to the first Finney Field. Turning left up the field boundary one could look over the wall into the 'Black Death'. This was a small field where victims of the cholera morbus epidemic of 1832 were buried in unconsecrated ground in an effort to prevent the spread of the disease. It is said that the bodies were buried here in quick lime. The gravestones erected there eventually came to lean against the boundary walls of the enclosure, and all would have been smashed to rubble when building began in 1965 had I not obtained two for garden decoration. Some of the houses on the eastern side of Hanbury Close are built upon this 'Black Death'.

Crossing the first Finney Field diagonally and crossing the top of the next, narrower field brought one to the foot of the great horse chestnut mentioned earlier, the finest single tree in the valley.

At the squeezer stile here, one path branched over the ridge to Cowley Lane, the other continued right, near the crest of the ridge in a westerly direction. Across this open land walked countless generations of Dronfield people, enjoying the broad vista across the valley and the wind straight out of the west. This way walked Leonard ('Tiptoe') Mitchell twice on Sundays to and from Cowley Mission, where he played the organ. I still see in my mind's eye Mr C. Bonser of Oxclose striking young swedes in the long field below the path in the heat of early summer and leaning against the wall to pass the time of day and have a moment's rest.

Farther along the ridge the path came near to the derelict Sloads House. Down in the valley to the north were the silver birches atop the Oxclose Colliery tips, and the distant chimney of Gosforth Colliery. In recent times the modern lines of Gosforth School were conspicuous across the fields, as was Gunstone's bakery. Today they are somewhat lost in the foreground lake of bricks, glass and concrete.

Down the old track northwards one reached, in a field's length, Oxclose Lane and the Gibbet Ash. Leftwards the lane forked left and over the ridge into Kitchen Wood; the right fork went up by Oxclose Farm to Dronfield Woodhouse. This fork of lanes was some yards to the south-east of the present junction of

Gosforth Drive with Hayfield Close.

Turning right at the Gibbet Ash, though, gave the lovely walk eastwards down the lane, deep hedged and tree hung. Now and then one glimpsed the spire of St John's church above the trees.

Where Gosforth Lane crossed the valley below Gosforth Colliery on a high, dry-stone embankment stood the town's former refuse-tip. Here, at tea-time, one was likely to see Frank Kirkland or Mr G. N. Woodhead driving the Manor Farm Friesian herd home for milking.

Along the lane walked some of the older inhabitants of this part of Dronfield. I particularly remember Mr Bonson, his bowler hat and a pair of smooth-haired fox terriers, Mr Shaw the watchmaker who lived at the westernmost house on old Gosforth Lane, who rode a motor-scooter into his eighties. He was something of a tyrant at home: if someone called to collect a watch he had been repairing, he would quickly turn his wrath on his timid second wife if she attempted to utter a word. "Oh, yes Mrs Shaw, have your say, my woman!" he would shout in front of the visitor, "Yes, ask Mrs Shaw and she will give you the answer for she knows all things. What is time? Mrs Shaw will tell you! What causes gravity? Oh yes, she can explain it!" he would sneer, pointing an accusing finger in her direction, much to everyone's embarrassment. Then there was Mr Dixon, father of Britain's best-known theatre-organist, who lived in later years with his daughter on Gosforth Lane. He had a bright and friendly face, and it was difficult to believe that he was an octogenarian. The residents hereabouts can no longer enjoy the peace and beauty which until recently lay so conveniently nearby.

I remember writing in July 1967 that a few days earlier I had looked for the last time over the lovely, summer valley from the windows of Gosforth School. That open view of fields, hills and the sky had been a constant attraction over the years, and with each passing season a kaleidoscope of colours had been revealed. No two summers gave quite the same pattern, no skies were repeated.

Over a long period the children have come and gone through the school, like those changing colours across the valley. Many of them remain only in the mind, as faces passing dream-like and no longer tangible. We may never see many of them again, or ever know what became of them, but I am sure that the lovely valley had a good effect on many.

It is sad to realize that in the years after 1967 this same countryside became covered with bricks, concrete and people. Only that ever-changing skyscape remains inviolate, with cloud-towers, broken isles of cumulus, or dark walls of purple-blue rain clouds, rain storms and crystal summer mornings. Those are the things I will always remember.

The Manor Farm fowls and muscovy ducks no longer cross the eastern end of the lane to the paddock beside the Baptist Chapel. The rustic loveliness has receded here as elsewhere in this once fertile and productive valley. One must now cross the desert-lands of tarmac and bricks and hurrying folk to reach the remaining paradise beyond that broad, southern ridge.

4

A Very Determined Woman

On a bright Sunday evening in spring, early in the 1920s, my aunts Joan and Mary Dearden walked along Cemetery Road, Dronfield towards Chesterfield Road and round to the back door of Midland House, close beside the railway lines. Climbing the steep steps, they knocked at the kitchen door and heard voices and a little subdued scuffling within; then the door was opened hesitantly to reveal Mrs Ward's slightly perturbed countenance and a shadowy figure snatching a plate of cold ham from the supper table and discreetly disappearing into the pantry with it.

Mrs Ward quickly regained her composure and invited the girls into the house, ushering them through the kitchen with haste and into the sitting-room. People occupying the Wards' station ought not really to have supper in the kitchen – at least, they ought not to be caught doing so by visitors like the Misses Dearden. Being Sunday there was a bit of fire glimmering faintly in the sitting-room grate.

"And how is your dear mother?" enquired Mrs Ward, gesturing the girls to be seated. Polite conversation proceeded, and as it did, the shadowy figure hovered in the background.

"Harold, perhaps Joan and Mary would like a little wine – get out the bottle!" Mrs Ward gestured again, this time to the sideboard. Her retiring son, Harold, did as he was told and brought round the drinks. "And, Harold, you may help yourself to a small glass, too," beamed his mother. Harold then resumed his position in the shadows near the door, ready for flight if necessary. It became obvious that mother and son were not really at ease, one or other of them glancing out of the window at intervals.

"Yes, Charlotte has gone over to Cowley, but she may be

34

back soon," said Mrs Ward presently, intimating that maybe it was time for their visitors to set off for home. Charlotte was the eldest daughter and by that time in the early twenties had shown that she had a mind of her own. She would most certainly have disapproved of the Dearden girls sipping wine in the sitting-room on Sunday evening when she was absent – Mrs Ward and Harold knew that there would be a 'scene' as soon as the visitors had departed if Charlotte arrived now. My aunts realized the situation and as quickly as good manners allowed set off for Hallowes Lane, luckily not meeting Charlotte on the journey.

Years later, when Harold was well into middle age, my Aunt Joan remembers that she saw him window-gazing in Chesterfield and, on going up to him, was told in a whisper as he glanced sidelong up and down the street, that "Charlotte's nearby", as if to say "Beware!"

Now Mrs Ward died in 1938, and one daughter married ("beneath her station") a railway ganger whom she had got to know when he worked on the main line behind Midland House. Charlotte took the reins with great purpose and moved herself – and Harold, of course – to a rambling Regency house called The Cliffe at the lower end of Green Lane, Dronfield. This had been the home of a Dr Samuel Rooth, JP, another well-known character of the town, though of an earlier generation. (Dr Rooth was born at Bridge House, Chesterfield in 1842 and was trained at several universities, including London, Paris and Vienna. He married the eldest daughter of the May family of Dronfield.)

As Charlotte grew older, she became even more purposeful and was noteworthy in the district for her love of protocol, for "the old and simple virtues of doing the right thing", as she once explained. As a landowner (the family, she always claimed, had held lands in the district for six hundred years), she knew the law, and she stuck to her guns with terrific tenacity. In later years no local authority or nationalized body was too powerful for her to tackle if and when she thought it necessary.

She was no small admirer of Doctor Samuel Johnson and agreed wholeheartedly with him that, "That fellow seems to me to possess but one idea, and that is a wrong one." In her case, such fellows were usually local and national authorities.

In 1960, for instance, she did battle with the Yorkshire Electricity Board and the GPO on the matter of wayleave, the passage of power and telephone lines over part of her estate. She fought both and won. Likewise, during World War II, she beat the local housing authority which claimed that one of her cottages at Cowley was empty and must be taken over for residential purposes. She immediately walked across the Finney Fields to the cottage and slept there, doing so for the rest of the war. Each morning she walked back to The Cliffe and lived there!

Most of Charlotte Ward's estate lay in the Unstone, Apperknowle and Cowley districts of north-east Derbyshire. Cowley is a truly pretty place, wood-girt and quiet and fairly hidden from the rest of the world. The lane that winds through it is still narrow, set between high hedges where dog roses bloom in summer. It comes twisting down south-westwards from Dronfield Hill Top and over the tiny stream which rises in Kitchen Wood (near Woodend Farm at the edge of the Gosforth Valley). It is a very small stream and has not even got a proper name; after winding beside Cowley Lane, it goes in the shadow of School Wood (former property of the Fanshawe family) and by Lee Bridge to skirt the western boundary of Monk Wood and joins the Barlow Brook downstream of the old bridleway bridge (also known as Lee Bridge) near the former Keeper's Cottage. But we are now some way from Cowley.

Cowley gets its name from the Old English words '*col*' and '*leah*', meaning 'the wood (or woodland clearing) where charcoal was burnt'. By 1315 the area was known as 'College', and the name slowly evolved to its present form. Newcomers to the district insist on referring to 'Cow-ly', but its origin clearly indicates that the natives are correct in their pronunciation of the word as 'Coaly'.

Spa House, originally the Big House of the district, stands close beside the lane to Dronfield. It was rebuilt in 1827 and so does not retain any of its older features. In the fields adjoining it there were three springs and two wells producing the finest and purest sulphurous water in this part of Derbyshire. At one time it was planned to develop Cowley as something of a spa (hence Spa House), but nothing ever came of the idea. Together with most of the property hereabouts, this was part of the Ward estate. Almost a mile nearer Holmesfield lies a rushy, ill-drained field called Cowley Gore which was owned by the family prior to 1666.

Only in recent years have the properties begun to change hands frequently, and consequently to have been much modi-fied and 'improved' so as to remove some of their native charac-ter. Perhaps the least spoilt house is Cowley Farm, near the little Cowley Mission where "Tiptoe" Mitchell was once the resi-dent organist (described in my *Peakland Days*, 1970). For many years during and after World War II, an old farmer called Andrews lived there. He always wore a large-brimmed hat and khaki puttees and worked his Shire horses in the fields running northwards towards Cowley Bottom and Hills Farm. In the end he retired to Holymoorside, but the farmhouse has been tastefully restored, an example to anyone intending to alter an old rural property. Across the lane from Cowley Farm stands Grange Farm, in those days the home of the Hitch family. This was the neatest and best-kept little holding in the district, and Mr Hitch was a well-known farmer, driving around the quiet countryside in an attractive brown float pulled by an equally good-looking chestnut horse. Every Friday afternoon he would go to Dronfield with one or other of his grown-up daughters to collect meal and grain from Fielding's shop near the railway station and groceries from shops in High Street. It is not so very long ago, but things have changed rapidly – the sight of that horse and float in the High Street would be a great curiosity today.

Charlotte Ward's short, stocky figure, thin greying hair pulled tightly back to a small, severe bun, was a familiar sight in the Cowley country. She would be seen quite regularly striding with some purpose, casting an eagle eye over her various properties. Tenants in the district must often have peeped anx-iously from behind their curtains at her passing, hoping that she had no reason for reprimand. If ever there was a complaint or a change of plan, Miss Ward was sure to win the day. Take, for instance, one of her last battles (in the sixties) against a well-known farmer called Nixon who was her tenant at Greenfield Farm, near the junction of Cowley Lane and Dobbin Lane. This well-to-do farmer had in some way broken his agreement with Miss Ward, and she decided to evict him. A hearing lasting several days took place at Cowley Mission, and the indefatigable spinster won her case. The unfortunate farmer had to leave Greenfield Farm, transferring his chattels to his other farm at Hasland.

At an earlier time the Water Board crossed swords with Miss Ward at her farm near the top of Unstone Hill. They knew that a manhole marked on their plans existed somewhere near the farmhouse, but one of their employees was unable to locate it, and when an official called at The Cliffe he was told that it was his business to find it, why should Miss Ward's time be wasted in doing his job for him? The puzzled official went to Unstone to look for himself but was likewise unsuccessful. In due course Miss Ward was asked to meet another official on the site and see what could be done to find the manhole. We can imagine Charlotte Ward enjoying the situation she found herself in, holding the trump card and smiling greatly at what she knew. The meeting took place at the appointed time, but the Water Board men were told in no uncertain terms that though the manhole did exist, they must find it for themselves. "Go back to your plans, look more carefully than before, and the truth will be revealed," she instructed them and returned home.

At last the penny dropped – the manhole was only a few yards from where the meeting had taken place, hidden beneath a large heap of cow manure. With the help of the tenant farmer, the heap was moved and the manhole revealed. Charlotte Ward liked that sort of incident, where she knew the answer and 'petty authority' was made to look slightly silly and incompetent.

At the beginning of World War II, Harold Ward went to live in Blackpool, away from the danger of German bombing raids, and Charlotte spent her time between The Cliffe and her cottage at Cowley. I was quite young when Harold returned home from Blackpool, and my first memory of him was when he came calling one sunny Saturday evening. He removed his black bowler hat as he entered our house, placed a rolled umbrella and raincoat on a hall chair and sat down somewhat nervously with us. I remember clearly the black suit, gold watch-chain and shining black boots; also the nervous mopping of his shining, bald brow from time to time.

In those later years Harold always answered the door at The Cliffe, usually sporting a green baize apron. "Have you an appointment to see Miss Ward?" he would enquire of the caller. If no appointment had been made, he would ask for a visiting-card. In the rare event of a card being presented, he would take a silver tray from the hall stand, place the card upon it and disappear into the shadows. Returning he would either send the caller away or ask him to enter and lead him to the sitting-room where his sister held her very proper interviews.

Some years ago I was talking to one of the country's foremost specialists in medals and coins at his shop in Cheltenham, and he told me the following story.

He one day received a letter from Miss Charlotte Ward stating that she had seen his advertisement for old coins in a magazine and wondered if he might like to see her collection. One or two very rare items were mentioned which aroused his interest. An appointment was made, and the dealer came north by train, changed to a bus at Chesterfield and eventually walked up the steps to the front door of The Cliffe. He remembered "a timid sort of butler with a green baize apron" opening the door and stating that Miss Ward was about to take lunch. Would he return in one hour. Away went the dealer, somewhat annoyed at this delay. He was directed to the Blue Stoops Inn in the High Street for refreshment and one hour later knocked once more on the front door of The Cliffe. This time he was shown to the sitting-room where Miss Ward sat at a large table with the coins laid out before her.

The collection looked most interesting and contained many coins which the dealer wanted. "Well, sir," said Charlotte when the coins had been examined, "What value do you put upon each coin? I want to know the current price of each one separately." The dealer was hoping to make an offer for the whole collection and thereby save much time and effort, but he went through each piece and gave what he thought was a fair price for every coin, Miss Ward writing down what he said.

"Thank you very much," she said when he had finished. "Well, Miss Ward, would you take a cheque for the coins?" the dealer asked, thankful that the hard work seemed to be done.

"A cheque? What for? I have no intention of selling any of

these coins!" came the firm reply, "I simply wanted to know the value of these coins for insurance purposes." And with that the dealer was shown to the door and left to make his way back to Cheltenham, a wiser man – and poorer to the tune of a return railway fare and one pub lunch!

"And that frightened little chap was her brother – not the butler?" he exclaimed when I told him, "Well, I'll give them full marks for fooling me!"

Charlotte's younger sister who had married a railway ganger had one child. After the premature death of this sister, Charlotte adopted the little girl, Mary. She was naturally an adored thing and the great light in her maiden aunt's life. When poor Mary died in her early twenties (in the 1950s) Charlotte was greatly affected and lost what faith she had in human nature. She turned increasingly to a love of animals. If she is remembered in the district as a bitter shrew who insisted on her own way, she must also be remembered as an ardent lover of animals who did much for their welfare in a positive way. A keen supporter of the League Against Cruel Sports, she often did battle with the Barlow Hunt. On one occasion a message reached her that this hunt was operating at Cowley and had been seen crossing her property, despite conspicuous notices forbidding trespass for the purpose of fox-hunting. She had someone drive her over to Cowley immediately, and, striding into one of her fields, she caught the huntsman retrieving the hounds which had strayed there. We can imagine the short, stiff figure squaring up to the mounted huntsman, and, raising her stick, she vowed that if he did not leave her land without delay, she would lay her stick across the horse's rump to no mean effect. Huntsman, hounds and the mounted field quickly moved onto Dobbin Lane and, as far as is known, never dared trespass on the Ward estate again.

Harold Ward died in February 1968, leaving £36,996, all of it to his sister. Charlotte lived on alone at The Cliffe for three more years. During that time I wrote to make an appointment to see her, hoping that she would help me with some facts of local history in the Cowley district. Her reply shows that there was a warm facet, a deep sympathy for what she considered deserving causes and people:

The Cliffe,
2 Green Lane,
Dronfield,
Nr. Sheffield.
10th March 1968

Dear Roger,

I knew you when you were a very small boy so we will not be on formal terms with each other, though we have not met for years.

My brother's death was a very sudden and a shattering experience. One thing we can be sure of and that is that our loved ones are very much better off out of this world than in it. My brother's dread was that he should survive me – we were very close to each other and I am pleased I was spared to take care of him, but I am very, very lonely. Mary gone and now my dear brother!

I shall be free after 4 pm on Friday, 15th instant when, unless I hear from you to the contrary, I will expect you to call.

Yours sincerely,
Charlotte M. Ward

On 15th March I rang the door bell at 4 pm, and Miss Ward opened the door to me. We had an interesting conversation for more than an hour.

"Of course, my boy, you will realize that I am something of a raconteur and enjoy nothing better than to talk of people and things to someone I know and respect," she explained. She also explained how experience had embittered her, that she had come to realize that animals were more faithful and appreciative than most humans.

"My poor cat was shot quite recently by vandals in my kitchen garden," she said, "That terrible act upset my brother, too – as did the shock he had not long ago when hooligans discharged an air-gun from Cliffe Park, through the kitchen window, directly above his head!" I imagined poor, trembling Harold mopping his brow and Charlotte striding out into the dark garden to threaten dire consequences upon the unseen intruders.

"The loss of so much of our front garden and the reduction of our privacy thereby upset Harold, too," she went on, "It was all too much for him."

Miss Ward was referring to the compulsory purchase of a strip of her front garden to allow the re-alignment of Callywhite

Lane. Even though she did lose that case, no one but she could have forced the local council to build a huge stone wall, all of twenty feet high, to retain her front garden after re-alignment. It is the most imposing piece of stone walling around any private house in this part of the country. Likewise, only the determination of Charlotte Ward forced the council to build a fine, drystone wall along the western side of the main road between Dronfield and the top of Unstone Hill, when that section of road was re-aligned. This included the preservation of a horse chestnut tree which would otherwise undoubtedly have been felled.

When Charlotte Ward died in March 1971, she left behind a Will which was totally expected in its complexity. She left £164,673 gross, including small amounts to "loyal and devoted servants and relatives" – and £100 for the upkeep of Dronfield Cemetery and the Ward family graves. The bulk of her estate she directed to be held in hand for at least five years after her death and the income from it to be given to the League Against Cruel Sports. Thereafter some real estate and "a fourth of the residue of the personal estate each to the RSPCA, at Dronfield, the National Anti-Vivisection Society in Sheffield and the People's Dispensary for Sick Animals, Heeley, Sheffield. The remainder of her real estate and a fourth of her personal estate went to the League Against Cruel Sports.

Forty acres of land near Apperknowle were included in the bequest to the League Against Cruel Sports, and a year after Charlotte Ward's death it was announced that local members of the League would patrol this territory on hunt days because this small area is "strategically placed and effectively gives protection to all wild life in an area of something like four thousand acres". The Master of the Barlow is reported to have told the Press that "We do not go into that area very much – the hunting is not very good."

Whatever the effect was, the 'no hunting' policy on this acreage and larger areas at Cowley maintained the ideals of a very determined woman. She had no political axe to grind against the hunting fraternity as some sections of the anti-hunting lobby have; hers was an absolute love of all animals and a great concern for their welfare which manifested itself in some very positive ways. It seems a pity that the scourge of inflation made it necessary for the RSPCA to sell a large part of the Cowley property in 1978.

Whenever I look across Green Lane to the darkened windows of The Cliffe beyond a fringe of laurels and towering sycamores I see in my mind's eye a short, upright figure striding out along a gravel path. Whenever I stray near School Wood or along the field paths near Cowley Mission I almost hear the rattle of the Hitchs' float along the lane, and the dim outline of that short, prim woman crossing her own acres with swinging arms – bound for Dronfield and ready for the next confrontation.

5

Henry Fanshawe's Legacy

The elaborate and colourful history of the Fanshawe family and their ancestral home in the parish of Holmesfield makes a good story. Few English families can trace the descent of a property in the direct line for almost seven centuries, but this has been possible with the Fanshawes because of the existence of the Holmesfield Court Rolls and the Wooley Charters in the British Museum.

It is not really certain whether the name Fanshawe originated as a place-name from which the family took their name or whether the place came to be named after the residents – 'Fanshawe's gate' or 'road'. Whatever its origin, the spelling of the name has evolved with time, from Faunchall and Fauncher to ffaunchelle and ffanshawe. The great family seat was called 'le Faunchallegatehede' in 1456, but from the early sixteenth century the family were called 'ffanshaw' or 'ffanshawe' (the latter spelling has prevailed since the eighteenth century).

Fanshawe Gate stands on the north-facing slope of the elevated ridge which separates the upper Vale of Barlow and the upper valley of the River Sheaf. At eight hundred feet above sea level it is not an ideal site, short of sunlight in winter and often hidden by hill mists; one wonders why the original settlers chose this particular site. Whatever the reason, there is evidence that the Fanshawes resided at Fanshawe Gate in 1260 and maybe from a considerably earlier date. They apparently leased land hereabouts from Beauchief Abbey at about this time, and it may be that the existence of these monastic lands is the reason for their living here, on this cold, northward-looking slope above the headwaters of the River Sheaf.

The Holmesfield Manor Roll of 1417 contains the first Fanshawe entry. It seems that it was the most powerful family in the district and that Fanshawe Gate was unquestionably the largest and most imposing mansion in the Dronfield area. Henry (or Robert) Fanshawe's eldest sons were John (born 1504) and Henry (born 1506), and this John succeeded his father in 1523. His brother Henry left the district and rose in rank to become Remembrancer to the Exchequer in 1566. This is a rather obscure and antiquated post now, but in the sixteenth century it was of considerable importance, involving the collection of all debts due to the Crown, supervision of fines imposed by the Star Chamber and reminding sheriffs of the subsidies to be collected from their respective counties, among several other duties.

While Henry had left Fanshawe Gate for the south, and later fame, in his late teens, his elder brother John lived the life of a yeoman farmer at Fanshawe Gate. At the dissolution of the monasteries in 1536 the tithes of all the local settlements from as far off as Hundall which had been due to the Premonstratensian abbey at Beauchief were granted to the Fanshawes here at Fanshawe Gate. The large tithe barn, over ninety feet long, which stands to the north of the present house, was probably built at this time to contain the corn paid in lieu of tithes.

Upon John Fanshawe's death in 1578, his eldest son, Thomas, inherited the family seat. He had succeeded his uncle Henry as Remembrancer to the Exchequer in 1568 and had already purchased Ware Park, Hertfordshire and other properties near London so sub-let Fanshawe Gate to his younger brother Robert. Robert Fanshawe brought up fourteen children, and all of them were said to have been well educated and to have gained good positions in life. It is also known that his uncle Henry (the first Remembrancer) and his elder brother, Thomas (the second Remembrancer), visited their relations at the old home above the Sheaf Valley at various times.

As already mentioned, the dwelling here was something of a great mansion. Harold Armitage states in his *Chantrey Land* (1910) that "even the most casual wanderer past Fanshawe Gate assumes that some house of more than ordinary pretensions has been built here" and goes on to describe the two fine sets of square stone pillars that were gate posts – "one set surmounted by the pine-cone ornament, the other by pyramids on balls". He goes on to suggest that they serve "for memorials of a time when a house stood here that was greater than any we may see in this place today", like the great gateway at Hazelbarrow, in the parish of Norton, which is a remnant of the former hall there (see Chapter 7).

After 1636 only younger branches of the family seem to have lived at Fanshawe Gate, and at about the same time work began to reduce the size of the mansion. A large amount of stone and timber went to Woodthorpe, down the lane towards Totley, for the erection of what is today Woodthorpe Hall. Many of the fine timbers exposed in the large attics at Woodthorpe are obviously second-hand, and it is logical to presume they came out of the roof of Fanshawe Gate in the seventeenth century. It is also recorded that the height of the house was reduced for some reason in 1825. What we see today is but a small portion of that great Fanshawe house, though its site is obvious, linking as it did the present remnant with the delightful tower-building across the garden often known as 'The Pigeon Cote'. Why so much of the house was removed is not known, though the reduced circumstances of this branch of the family may have something to do with it.

The most illustrious member of the Fanshawe family was Sir Richard, born at Parsloes, in Essex, in 1608 and grandson of Thomas, second Remembrancer. Richard was a brilliant scholar and entered Jesus College, Cambridge at the age of fifteen. In 1626 he entered the Inner Temple and between 1632 and 1635 travelled abroad extensively. In 1635 he accompanied Lord Aston to Madrid and so began a long association with Spain. Nine years later, at the age of thirty-six, he was made Secretary of War to the fourteen-year-old Prince of Wales, at a particularly tricky period for such a position in England. Throughout the Civil War he was active in the service of Charles I and in 1645 was nominated to be Resident in Spain. During the years of strife he travelled extensively to France and to Ireland and for his trouble was created a baronet in 1650. His wife was the determined Lady Ann Fanshawe who is best remembered for her useful and interesting memoirs (*The Memoirs of Lady Ann Fanshawe*, originally transcribed under her supervision and published in 1676. A new edition of 1829–30 was reprinted by Bodley Head in 1907). Sir Richard died in Madrid in 1666, but Lady Ann lived on until 1680.

The Fanshawe family history is complicated somewhat by the fact that Thomas Fanshawe, second Remembrancer, married twice. By his first wife, Mary Bourchier, his eldest son became Sir Henry Fanshawe, third Remembrancer, and it was he that succeeded to Fanshawe Gate in 1601. His son was Sir Thomas Fanshawe, created Viscount Fanshawe of Dromore, Ulster, in 1661. Four viscounts succeeded in turn, but the fourth and fifth ones were bachelor brothers (they were, incidentally, eighth and ninth Remembrancers respectively) and so the title became extinct in the eighteenth century. Ownership of Fanshawe Gate passed to the descendants of Thomas Fanshawe's second marriage, the Fanshawes of Parsloes, Essex.

Then, in March 1825, Charles Robert Fanshawe created a mortgage on the estate for a period of five hundred years, but after 102 years Basil Thomas Fanshawe regained the property. Today this lovely old farmhouse in the shadow of the high moors is the home of Cynthia and John Ramsden, a most satisfactory state of affairs when one realizes what Henry Fanshawe, first Remembrancer, provided for in his last Will, dated 1st September 1567.

Though this influential Elizabethan had only occasionally returned to the district of his birth, he must obviously have maintained strong sentimental and family links with it because in this Last Will he made provision for the establishment of a school in the parish of his birth (Holmesfield was then a part of Dronfield parish). His nephew Thomas Fanshawe, second Remembrancer, had the job of putting his uncle's wishes into effect and obtained a charter for the new school from Queen Elizabeth I in 1579.

The original School House was built about 1580 overlooking what has long been known as Fanshawe Bank, near the upper end of Church Street, Dronfield. This building still exists much as it was built, though the windows were much enlarged in Georgian times; it consisted of a schoolroom and headmaster's dwelling.

In 1731 the Usher's House was erected nearby, beside Church Street, and this, likewise, remains unaltered to this day. Its red-brick construction has given rise to the popular name 'Red House'. The Usher was the assistant master and, particularly in the eighteenth century, he virtually ran the school. Above the front door is a large inscribed tablet, its Latin text meaning: "For the perpetual use of the Assistant Master of the Grammar School of Sir Henry Fanshawe, the inhabitants of Dronfield built this house by voluntary subscription in the year of our Lord 1731".

For nine years in the middle of the nineteenth century a member of the Fanshawe family served as headmaster, but he proved to be an absentee, living in the south and paying Dr E. Y. Haslam to act for him. In 1866 this Dr Haslam became headmaster, and the following year the new buildings over-looking the Sheffield-Chesterfield turnpike were occupied, the old core of the present school. These substantial buildings cost £1,989.10.0, and the place was soon afterwards described as "a pseudo-Elizabethan façade with nothing behind it", presumably a sarcastic attack on Waller K. Bedingfield, the new head-master appointed to succeed Dr Haslam in 1869.

The powers of the Fanshawe family in the running of the school came to an end in 1888 when Charles Chapman Bag-galey became headmaster. The Bedingfields continued to live at the old School House, and many Dronfield people can still remember Mr Bedingfield as a very old man, a shadowy, whis-kered figure often seen by the children who attended the private school run by his two daughters, Miss Bessie and Miss Edith, in the original schoolroom. This little school existed through the first quarter of this century; later the Misses Bedingfield were Dronfield's Registrars.

Charles Chapman Baggaley was headmaster for thirty-eight years up to 1926. He lived in the purpose-built headmaster's residence which occupied the western part of the new school; his wife prepared the meals for day pupils and boarders alike, a sort of matron-cum-cook-housekeeper. The teaching staff con-sisted of the headmaster, an assistant and a drill instructor. A family called Hall lived at the adjoining New Hall and ran a timber merchant's business from the yard beside it. Mr Bag-galey is best remembered as a founder member of the Hallowes Golf Club which occupied fields belonging to the old farm called Hallowes Farm at the top of Hallowes Lane, the ancient route to Chesterfield. He is also remembered by old pupils as something of a tyrant and bully who thought nothing of kicking

Unstone Viaduct in the Drone Valley south of Dronfield. The spire of Dronfield parish church is in right distance (Chapter 2).

Glasshouse Hill (664 feet) from the hill path above Unstone (Chapter 2).

Summerley Hall,
rebuilt after 1650,
high above the eastern
slopes of the Drone
Valley (Chapter 2).

In the copse behind
Hall Farm, High
Street, Dronfield in
1966 (Chapter 2).

Farwater Lane, Dronfield, in 1960. (Chapter 2)

At the bottom of Farwater Lane, Dronfield, winter 1952 (Chapter 2).

One of Captain Horace Grainger's excavations beside the Lea Brook, Gosforth Valley, showing a 'skull stone' on a shelf in 1957 (Chapter 3).

One of the cholera graves at Summer Green above the Gosforth Valley before housing development began in 1966 (Chapter 3).

Oxclose Farm in the upper Gosforth Valley on the day before demolition in 1971 (Chapter 3).

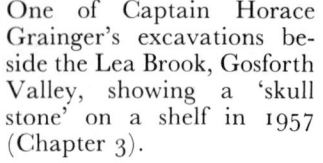

Captain Horace Grainger in Coal Aston Wood, about 1955
(Chapter 3).

The Cliffe, Green Lane, Dronfield, from Henry Fanshawe School, spring (Chapter 4).

The gateway at Fanshawe Gate, Holmesfield. (Chapter 5)

The Victorian south front of Henry Fanshawe School, Dronfield. (Chapter 5)

Cordwell Bridge after
the height of the flood,
July 1973. (Chapter 6)

The old gateway to
Hazelbarrow Hall,
Norton. (Chapter 7)

The south front of The Oakes-in-Norton from the park. (Chapter 7)

The old post office at Norton. (Chapter 7)

a small boy the length of a classroom if he got an algebraic cal-
culation wrong – it happened to my father, and he suffered a
back injury for the rest of his life!

Probably the best known pupil of Charles Baggaley's later
years is George Houghton, golf addict, artist and author. He
lived in Paris for twelve years between 1926 and 1937, working
for the *Daily Mail* as foreign correspondent. Returning to England just before the last war, he quickly joined the RAF and
took over a unit in the Western Desert. Later he joined Lord
Tedder's personal staff, became a Group Captain and was
awarded an OBE.

Since 1945 George Houghton has specialized in writing
light-hearted golf books, drawing cartoons and doing work for
radio and television. In all he has written forty-six books, and
he and his wife have travelled the world to do books such as *Golf
Addict in Gaucho Land* and *Golf Addict Goes East*. His memories of
Dronfield Grammar School go like this:

My period at Dronfield was 1915 to 1922. Taking in most of the
First World War I suppose was colourful enough. There was something quite unusual and to some extent 'different' about Dronfield,
with our very pro-French Head. Charles C. Baggaley wore an
imperial beard, was considered a bit of a lad and took French to the
top forms and regaled them with wonderful stories of his regular
twice-a-year trips to France. The last time I saw him was, I suppose, in the early thirties when, having retired, he had taken on the
Secretaryship of the Hallowes Golf Club. He was a very tweedy
cigar/port aroma-ed man, and certainly a character whom one
would never forget. He put a stamp of originality on our school
which I think we all secretly enjoyed.

During my days we had some quite outstanding pupils, though
not particularly from a high scholastic point of view. The only chap
I remember who did very well at University and Further Education
was Harold Oldman, who went on to be a Principal Education
Officer for York. The outstanding sportsman of those days was un-
doubtedly Roy Goodall, a scholarship lad from Dronfield Woodhouse. In a cricket match against Dronfield town I once remember
seeing him drive four successive balls over a very high elm tree at
the bottom of the field, finishing up in 'Boss Bag's' garden. The
tree must certainly have gone now, and I don't suppose you are
using that sports field.

The upper part of this field, incidentally, during the Great War had been dug over by pupils to grow vegetables, and instead of games, physical exercises, etc, we had to work the allotment, which didn't please most of us. One quite outstanding incident during my time occurred in the old dining-hall. May Baggaley, Boss Bag's kind and charming wife, used to supervise the cooking for a limited number of boarders in those days, but also, of course, the dining-room was used by all pupils who stayed for lunch, although most of us – anxious to use every available moment on the games field – would bring packed lunches from home. During the brief time when I was a boarder, and following disagreeable odours emanating from under the dining-hall, floor boards were taken up. Generations of pupils, when their food displeased them, had been emptying oddments into a hole in the floor. I am not sure whether this went merely into the foundations, or a basement cellar, but the practice had certainly gone on for many years because when a team of men with shovels and picks eventually had to come to clear away the compressed and rotted throw-aways (it was about ten feet deep over a goodish sized area), all manner of interesting things were found, including, I remember, a George III pewter drinking-tankard, and ancient exercise-books going back into the nineteenth century.

The masters in those days were Frank Cade, who I remember first came to the school with his new bride; he was very smart in a captain's uniform, and his wife Doris wore a great purple boa. Frank Cade took over the senior mastership from 'Pip' Baldwin, an irascible chap who could land out a few slaps when he felt like it. The other great pillar of Dronfield Grammar School throughout my period was, of course, Miss Lilian Spaven, who taught art and had charge of the juniors. She was the most beloved person I have ever met. To her do I owe my early inclination towards drawing, and when I left school she quickly got me installed doing a three-nights-a-week stint at Sheffield Art School. Being war time, we had a great number of women teachers, then after the war one by one they were replaced by folk like Messrs Preece, Thomas and Evanson. Also I remember we had a strange character named Knapp, undoubtedly of oriental extraction. Also, there was 'Horace' Johnson, an English master who later went to take over a school in Old Sarum.

During my latter years at Dronfield I brought out and edited *The Dronfeldian*, which was our most humble school magazine in those days.

In 1926 Charles Baggaley retired and built a house, 'Penmore', close to his beloved Hallowes club-house. He was succeeded by Norman Shera Millican, a graduate of University College, Oxford. He made his home at New Hall, adjacent to the school. In the twenty-seven years of his headmastership the school can be said to have enjoyed its Golden Age; a period when there were more pupils and a nucleus of well-liked, long-serving staff. Dronfield Grammar School, as it was by that time known, was a happy school with an almost family atmosphere with N. S. Millican at its head – a dramatic character with a true sense of what well-balanced education was all about.

It was this headmaster who claimed to be the only person to have climbed to the weathervane atop Dronfield parish church spire (132 feet) and to that upon the school tower; on the latter he actually sat cross-legged! Those who were his pupils can imagine what he would have said and done if any of them had dared to do such a thing.

The school had grown physically in Charles Baggaley's time, and in the thirties the quadrangle was formed by attractive brick, concrete and timber wings on the eastern, northern and western sides. It was in post-war years that I came to this world of DGS, a world which from the start impressed itself upon me by its lightness and brightness and the wealth of large pictures about the place. It is those vistas of other worlds – prints by Montague Dawson in the dining-room, by Stanhope Forbes and others in corridors and classrooms – that remain as the clearest memories of happy school days – those pictures and some of the staff.

Several generations of Dronfeldians can never forget Harold Preece and those terrifying chemistry lessons, Jack Dodd with his tattered gown conducting singing lessons, with Miss Doreen Darley in the dining-room while 'the kitchen ladies' chattered loudly behind. Miss Darley came in 1926 and was senior mistress for so many years. She made her art lessons very interesting to those of us with leanings that way. She, more than any other teacher, generated an interest in the world of fine arts which has grown with the years.

A particular memory remains of woodwork lessons in the workshop below the dining-room (now the library). Whenever George Allen left us to get on with an exercise during our Fifth Year, we would plunge into battle, taking cover behind benches as pieces of scrap wood were hurled – and on more than one occasion chisels were thrown, to vibrate loudly in bench-tops close to one's ears. A look-out would shout "He's coming!", and everyone would rapidly resume work. Once, I remember, a piece of wood was thrown and smashed a light bulb. The glass was quickly swept up while the culprit raced into the store-room to find a replacement. He found one and, standing upon a bench, attempted to fix the new bulb in the socket. Unfortunately he did not seem to know how this was done, thinking it screwed into place. The look-out gave his cry and everyone raced to his place to resume normal working.

"What's been going on?" asked George menacingly, suspecting the silence and over-zealous industry of his pupils. There was no need for any answer because at that moment the bulb fell from its socket and smashed on the bench below. The offender admitted everything, and no more was said. I think our battles in the workshop ended soon afterwards.

George Allen came to be a colleague and good friend in later years, a native of Dronfield who knew so much about his town and the people in it. As I write this chapter, news comes of his sudden death (1978); and with the passing of the years fewer of that happy family remain.

Harold Preece died in 1960, Mr Thomas in 1960, Mr Dodd in 1962, Miss Darley in 1972, Mr Millican in 1974, Mr Dixon in 1977. Miss Webley and Mr Hayton have also died. Others well remembered by so many remain, of course, as a link with a happy school. Miss Riggs and Miss Gardner come immediately to mind.

Miss I. O. Gardner came to Dronfield Grammar School in 1930 to teach French. She remained until retirement in 1969, succeeding Miss Darley as Senior Mistress. Though a native of Gloucestershire, she is considered by all her friends as a Dronfeldian – to the extent that she is "considering being buried in Dronfield". She is one of those active, purposeful, outgoing sorts who never wastes a minute of her days and is liked by all who know her for that very drive and a warm humanity which seems so rare in this modern world. "If you want something doing, ask a busy person" is very much a truism where Miss Gardner is concerned. Guiding and scouting have long been her concern; an accomplished oboe player and keen and knowledgeable gardener, one wonders how she ever fitted in the demands of a successful career. Her home is at Highgate, high on the hill above the town and close to the golf course where Charles Baggaley spent so much time.

In 1956 Dronfield Grammar School reverted to become 'Henry Fanshawe School', and in 1965 it became a senior comprehensive school, taking pupils from the age of fourteen years. Now the school has large extensions, one thousand pupils and seventy teaching staff; and that should be the end of the story.

There is one interesting fact remaining. Though the school founded by the Will of Henry Fanshawe four centuries ago has changed out of almost all recognition, the Foundation Governors still exist as trustees of the investments made from the sale of properties and land left for the endowment of the school. It is the duty of the Foundation Governors "to conserve and improve the capital and to use the income for the benefit of the school". The Chairman of the Statutory Governors is John Ramsden who, like Cynthia, his wife, is an old pupil of the school. They now live at Fanshawe Gate, an arrangement of which I am certain Henry Fanshawe would approve.

6

Coal-Measure Valleys in Winter and Summer

There are, luckily, some parts of the south Pennine flanks quite undiscovered by the hordes; may they long remain quiet and untrodden; may this chapter not help to spoil their peace, their undiscovered loveliness.

The country I have in mind extends as a borderland down the eastern side of Peakland, separating the high gritstone country from the productive coal-measures of the Rother Valley. It is ridge-and-valley territory, punctuated by woods and drained by quiet streams.

There is the Barlow Brook and all its lesser and greater tributaries, the Linacre Brook and the River Hipper and its tributaries. The interesting thing about the Barlow Brook itself, greatest tributary of the River Drone described in Chapter 2, is that it has several names for different sections of its course. Millthorpe Brook is the name given to it upstream from Millthorpe. Between Millthorpe and Barlow Commonside it is called Dunston Brook, and only downstream of Commonside (to the confluence with the Drone near Sheepbridge Works) is it properly Barlow Brook.

The interesting thing is that the section called Dunston Brook is all of two miles above the site of Dunston, near Sheepbridge Works. This little settlement, incidentally, is first recorded in the early years of the twelfth century as 'Donston', literally 'Dunn's farm'. It seems likely that the man whose name was attached to the settlement gave it also to the stream, but why has the name come to be used only for that short section upstream of Barlow Commonside and downstream of Millthorpe?

Mention of the Millthorpe district reminds me of one of its most attractive tributaries which flows north-eastwards from the high pastures about Moorhall, through Rose Wood and out into the valley bottom to join the Dunston Brook below Millthorpe's ford. It is called Pingle Dike, deriving from the Middle English *'pingel'*, meaning 'a small enclosure' – hence, a rivulet draining a small enclosure. But where is this small enclosure? There are so many lesser fields today, since wholesale enclosure two centuries ago.

Rearing at the head of the Vale of Barlow, at its very focal point, is a huge whale-back of a hill, quite symmetrical when seen from the east, and clothed all this century in mainly coniferous plantation. Seen from the high ground to the west, particularly from the Owler Bar–Baslow main road half a mile south of Owler Bar, the slopes of this dome are not so high but nonetheless very regular and tree-covered. This is Smeekley Wood, and the name can be found recorded as early as 1364, when it was 'Smeclif'. By 1497 it had evolved to 'Smeykeclyff', both names derived from Old English terms for 'smooth, steep slope'. The covering of wood seems to have developed by the late-seventeenth century – there is a reference to 'wood at Smeakly' in 1699. But what is the origin of this unusual land form, here at the boundary of the coal measures and millstone grit?

All this intricate landscape bordering the eastern fringe of Peakland consists of scarp and dip landforms built up of a number of escarpment units. Smeekley's present 'dome' is really a structurally determined outlier of Green Moor rock (Green Moor is a tiny settlement between Stocksbridge and Thurgoland where this particular coal-measure stratum was identified) in the composite cuesta belt of this district.

The consequent streams which flow here eastwards down the dip slope and join at the eastern foot of Smeekley to become the Barlow Brook, and their subsequent tributaries, have picked out the structural weakness here and aided the erosion which has formed this fascinating landform. On a warm and sunny August afternoon Rod Brown, of the Geography Department of Sheffield University, and I walked upon Smeekley and, standing at the little col which joins the hump-backed hill to the moorland immediately to the west, the remarkably smooth twenty-five to thirty-degree slope on the south side could be seen as a continuation of the extensive scarp slope extending below Birks Farm towards Leash Fen, facing westwards towards Ramsley and Big Moors. It is quite possible that a fault exists on the north-west side of Smeekley, near the col just mentioned.

All this western and southern side of the dome is clothed with mature deciduous woodland, largely beech. The rest of the hill has a dense planting of conifers, and, high up on the eastern side, a square plot of deciduous trees turns grass-green in spring and coppery-gold in October.

Most of the pretty, hidden side-streams in this country above the main east-west valleys have a nick-point, a place where the water reaches softer rock and through centuries has worn away its course at a more rapid rate. Such nick-points produce, in fact, waterfalls of modest size. One can find them concealed in the upper reaches of most of the tributary valleys but my particular favourites are a lichen-covered, little fall in Bank Wood, immediately to the south of Linacre Middle Reservoir, and a surprisingly high rock step upstream of Crowhole Reservoir, where the brook tumbles through Grange Wood east of Grangewood and Grangelumb Farms.

All this complicated countryside is enhanced by deep snow-fall, and the Big Snow of early 1947 was an exciting time for a schoolboy. Heavy snowfall always beautifies and silences our surroundings, and for weeks I walked down High Street and Church Street, Dronfield to the Grammar School through an old-world setting. Ivy House stood empty in the lower part of High Street, and I well remember the tall, white crests of the drifts leaning level with the top of the bay windows and the front door. Mrs Sykes seemed always to be peering from the doorway of the Red Lion Inn at the bottom of Church Street, peering out over the piled snow, asking children to run to the shop for her.

There was, of course, relatively little transport at that time, and the few bread-vans and cars delivering milk which came up and down High Street and Church Street ran smoothly and quietly on the packed snow.

The heaviest fall came on a day in the middle of February, when three feet nine inches fell. It was about that date that my father and I built a large igloo in the back garden. It lasted for many weeks, and we had a primus stove inside to boil water. We made cups of tea, and it got surprisingly warm inside when everyone came in for refreshment.

Farwater Lane descended from the Corn Laws Monument in High Street into the valley and then climbed to Dronfield Hill Top (its upper section still exists as Gosforth Lane). This lane was totally blocked by deep snow after several of the blizzards. I well remember the horse-drawn snowplough cutting a narrow track through the drifts. Local farmers were contracted to the County Council to operate snowploughs whenever necessary, using their heavy horses and men. The snow was so deep in 1947 that most of the ploughs in use near Dronfield were drawn by two, or even three, heavy horses. What a sight it was – the steam spurting from distended nostrils as the Shires strained at their chains on the steep climb to Hill Top.

The drifts at the Hyde Park Inn covered the signpost at the cross-roads, and the gas lamps up there on the ridge were almost inundated. By early March Farwater Lane and Cowley Lane were narrow gorges cut through the crusted snow which was piled to a height of twenty feet on either side.

One memorable Saturday we walked by Barlow Lees to Peakley Hill and saw the roof of the old, wooden Youth Hostel there peeping from a deep drift beside the lane. On the way home to Dronfield the sky was clear and there was not a sound in all the world, except for the crunching of our feet as another severe frost took hold of the night. The moon came up and illuminated the country as we passed through the shadows of the great drifts.

More than twenty-six years later this part of the world experienced another sort of extreme weather, when a complex trough of low atmospheric pressure drifted over north Derbyshire and came to a stop for more than twenty-four hours. Saturday 14th July 1973 became drizzly during late morning as we unloaded baled hay at Unthank Lane Farm. The sky brightened a little to allow some more baling during the afternoon, but as I walked through Monk Wood and on below Bull Close Farm that evening, dark blue clouds lay piled on the western horizon, and before I had regained the old bridge over the Barlow Brook near the Keeper's Cottage, heavy rain had begun to fall. The sky looked particularly angry.

It rained all night and continued all the next day, with some heavy downpours. My five-mile walk across the Linacre Valley and through Rose Wood saw me soaked by the deep and bending bracken. There was no reduction in the forceful downpour as I retraced my steps during the evening. Each of the streams I crossed was swollen out of recognition, and the Pingle Dike had become a raging, chocolate torrent which was traversed only with care. The trickle at the foot of the slope below Barlow Woodseats Hall had become a swirling, muddy whirlpool, as had the Sud Brook at Jumble Hole, down the fields to the north of Ingmanthorpe. Again, the rain continued through Sunday night.

In the two days of that weekend this part of the country received almost seven inches of rain – a quantity that would fall in twelve normal summer weeks. In the upper reaches of Derwent Dale 5·27 inches fell on Sunday 15th July 1973, and this is the second highest daily rainfall figure ever to be recorded in Derbyshire. The shores of Barbrook Reservoir, near Owler Bar, recorded 4·27 inches, and at Birley Farm, at the head of the Linacre Valley, 3·83 inches fell on the same day.

As I have said, it rained right through Sunday night. Some unusual places were flooded. The cross-roads where Clod Hall Lane intersects the Baslow-Sheffield road was blocked by a thundering cataract which issued from Leash Fen, and an extensive lake formed in the little valley of Bar Brook towards the reservoir. The Barlow Brook became a powerful river and flooded all the low-lying fields between Smeekley and Sheepbridge.

At the height of the flood the arch of Cordwell Bridge disappeared. The pretty ford at Millthorpe was completely hidden by a mass of deep water, logs and sodden bracken. The substantial railings alongside the ford were smashed and twisted by the force of the water, and remain so to this day. Ironically a reliable water supply seems to have been an old problem at Millthorpe for an old pipe still runs underground from the waterspout in Millthorpe Lane down to the vicinity of the ford, serving Mill Farm. Old waterpipes criss-cross the Home Field at Unthank Lane Farm, remnants of earlier attempts to get a decent supply to Mill Farm. An overflow from a trough at Unthank Lane Farm was put underground right down to Mill

Farm years ago, but this provided a supply only if the upper farm had a surplus! The late Mrs Ebbie Richardson used to recount attempts by Millthorpe cottagers to get the best of an unreliable supply for washdays. Seymour Shepley recalls Mrs Richardson's amusing tales of these folk deepening their wells, "digging against each other by night".

On the morning of Monday 16th July 1973 Millthorpe residents had too much of the stuff; and two miles downstream the Walker family were experiencing serious problems at Monkwood Farm. A four-foot torrent suddenly swept through the yard at 7.45 am as two of the farmer's sons were milking. Water poured into cowsheds and soon threatened to drown the terrified cows tied at their standings. The two men managed to release these animals and drove them to higher ground, but a dozen calves were almost submerged in another shed. Quickly they were tied by their necks with a rope and pulled through the chest-high water to a slope above the yard. Three feet of muddy water swirled through the house, eight milk churns were carried off and a large proportion of the recently harvested hay was damaged or destroyed.

A similar flood had affected Monkwood Farm fifteen years previously and the major cause of both incidents was the confined space under the bridge immediately downstream. This has since been rebuilt with much more room for flood waters to get away – the Walkers should now sleep more easily in their beds in times of torrential rain.

All that week rain and showers continued, but the land slowly dried out.

Three years later the same valleys were silent and burning in the phenomenal drought which had many of the features of pre-monsoon conditions in the Deccan of peninsular India. There was great heat and no rainfall from early June. This sort of weather was experienced throughout much of our islands, but it is interesting to recall some of the facts as they affected the southern Pennines in particular.

During early July temperatures were daily in the nineties. At teatime on Monday 12th July there was a heavy electrical storm with heavy rain for half an hour. Thereafter there was no rain whatsoever until 28th August (though a little rain was recorded in parts of Derbyshire on 30th July). As August passed, temperatures fell a little; in late August they were in the low eighties each day on the lower ground in northernmost Derbyshire.

The first rain to break the long drought came between 28th and 31st August (0·15 inches were recorded for these four days at Wingerworth, near Chesterfield), and this brought much cooler, clearer weather thereafter. By early September it was forecast that at least six inches of rainfall were needed to supply the soil of north Derbyshire with sufficient water before there would be any appreciable run-off to give life again to the streams and to start the long process of filling reservoirs. One most noticeable effect of the long drought was the tired look of the country; deciduous trees began to lose their leaves one month before normal, and one roadside horse chestnut at the top of Unstone Hill became dusty-gold early in September and almost leafless by the end of the month. Autumnal quiet had reigned upon this district of gentle, intricate hills all summer through. Birdsong was minimal, and the lively splash of falling water was not heard in the woods from June to September.

7

A City Belvedere and Chantreyland

When the eighteen-year-old J. M. W. Turner was sent by Walker, the publisher, to Derbyshire and neighbouring counties to make topographical drawings he travelled northwards to Sheffield by the coach from London. The year was 1793. His first sight of the town would be from the top of the steep ground immediately to the north of Norton village, where the old main road (Derbyshire Lane) skirted Meersbrook Park. It has been suggested that Turner knew instinctively that he was not likely to find a better belvedere of Sheffield than this, with that sudden, broad vista over the Sheaf Valley to the major buildings of the town centre, with Shirecliffe and Wincobank Hill in the background. Whether he searched the high ground around the town for a better viewpoint is not recorded, but, in the end, he came back to the edge of Meersbrook Park and produced his drawing which ultimately appeared in *The Itinerant*, and this was later reissued as *The Copper Plate Magazine* of 1798.

Sheffield is the highest city of its size in Europe (the city's western boundary reaches 1,502 feet at High Neb on Stanage Edge) and is more closely surrounded by hills and steep ground than any other industrial city in Britain. Although there are many good viewpoints, this one on the southern side at Meersbrook is generally accepted as being the finest because it is well lit by a rearward sun for most of the day and is sufficiently close to the city centre to reveal details of industry and architecture, easily recognizable features such as St George's church, Portobello of 1825, the Town Hall of 1896, some of the University buildings and the recent, tree-girt Hallam Tower Hotel. None of these featured, of course, in Turner's drawing, but the parish church (raised to the rank of cathedral when Sheffield became a city in 1914) was a part of the view he had from the edge of Meersbrook Park. The characteristic crocketed spire of the early-fifteenth-century parish church would have been the most conspicuous skyline feature of the town two centuries ago.

Other artists chose this area for their work. David Martin's engraving of 1791 looked the same way but from much lower down the slope, beside the old Heeley Tilt Mill dam. The father of Richard Parkes Bonington produced a similar view in 1801, and Thomas Hofland's picture of 1826 was from higher up in Meersbrook.

Meersbrook House is a red-brick mansion built about 1780 by Benjamin Roebuck, one of the sons of the Sheffield cutler and industrialist John Roebuck. The Roebucks later fell on hard financial times, and the Shore family followed them on this estate. The Shores likewise 'suffered financial reverses', and Meersbrook House became the property of the Milners; then, in 1890, it was opened by the Earl of Carlisle as the Ruskin Museum of the Guild of St George. The fine collection of rare minerals, natural history items and works of art was originally given to help "educate and enlighten the working classes" of this once dark and dirty industrial town. It was originally housed in Upper Walkley on the north-western side of Sheffield. In a guidebook of 1899 the ornithological collection, primarily the celebrated Eyton Collection, was believed to be the most complete set of coloured bird illustrations and drawings in existence. Most of the drawings and paintings were produced for this museum by artists trained by Ruskin, and, appropriately, the original sketch by J. M. W. Turner of that best view of Sheffield from near the top of the park was included. By 1953 the decline in numbers of visitors to the museum caused it to be closed, and the Ruskin Collection was transferred to Sheffield City Museum, Library and Art Gallery. Meersbrook House is now the headquarters of Sheffield Corporation Recreation Department.

Up at the top of Meersbrook Park, close to the place where the view of Sheffield is at its best, stands the Bishops' House. This is a fourteenth-century half-timbered building erected on a massive stone base. Such black-and-white structures are now rare in this part of England, and this is the best example remaining on the eastern flanks of the south Pennines. Centuries ago, when oak, straw and reeds were readily available on the lower ground, there were many half-timbered and thatched-roofed dwellings. They were largely replaced by stone and, as manufacturing spread, by easily-made bricks. Look down towards Heeley in the Sheaf Valley, and the packed houses of Victorian and Edwardian development are evidence of the wealth accumulated by brick-makers at that time.

Why is this lovely old building alongside Norton Lees Lane called 'the Bishops' House'? The ancient family of Blythe are enduringly remembered as Norton residents by the Blythe Chapel in Norton parish church. William Blythe's monument occupies the Blythe Chapel; it is known that he had a coat-of-arms in 1485, and two of his five sons became bishops. It is likely that the half-timbered house we see today at Norton Lees was the home of William Blythe and his family. John was the elder of the two who rose to fame. He became Warden of King's Hall, Cambridge in 1488, later Master of the Rolls and in 1494 was consecrated Bishop of Salisbury. Other posts he occupied were Chancellor of Cambridge University and Chancellor of Ireland. He died in 1499 and was buried behind the high altar of Salisbury Cathedral. The younger brother was Geoffrey. He was educated at Eton and Cambridge, where he followed John as Warden of King's Hall in 1498. In 1502 Henry VII sent him on diplomatic work to Hungary, and on his return in 1503 he became Bishop of Lichfield and Coventry. It was Geoffrey Blythe who founded his family's chantry chapel in Norton church. So, you see, the old half-timbered house at the top of Meersbrook Park has good reason to be called 'the Bishops' House' for two were probably born therein. It is scheduled as an Ancient Monument and is open as a museum at certain times.

The steep and wooded valley which falls away to the east of Meersbrook Park is the Meersbrook Valley, once a truly rural backwater initially unaffected by the industrial development which spread up the Sheaf Valley in early and mid-Victorian times. Its lower reaches were called Rushdale, before the stream ran on through the bottom of Meersbrook Park, which was, according to Harold Armitage in 1910, "a glen of unusual

beauty" with great oaks comparable with any in the north Mid-
lands. The eminent naturalist Charles Dixon spent all his early
years on this side of Sheffield and had permission from the Milners to visit any part of Meersbrook Park. He knew Heeley and
Meersbrook before the Midland Railway came in the 1870s,
and in his *Annals of Bird Life* of 1890 he was writing with feeling
of old Rushdale as "My ruined aviary!" He knew every corner
and tree there, but by 1910 it had changed completely, and
Harold Armitage was describing the oaks and beeches and
melodious songs of birds replaced by "tuneless groves of drying
clothes". The bell of a new school was clanging, too, and
"where in days that are gone beyond recall we had the scent of
the wild rose, arises now the pungent odour of a pickle factory".

Yes, the lower Meersbrook Valley (Rushdale) was soon
swallowed up by urban sprawl. Higher up, to the south-east, the
valley bottom remained fairly unspoilt until quite recent years.
Two ancient farms stood well up the slope to the west of the
stream, fine old buildings associated with hard-working
yeoman stock. Lees Hall was largely a seventeenth-century
stone house added to older property. The names of the occupants of this farm make an interesting list for they are largely
the names of families living within a dozen miles of Meersbrook. Widow Cave married John Bright of Dronfield about
1680; William Wastnidge was occupier in 1691. By 1693
Edward Greenwood was living there, and his wife was Beathea,
daughter of Andrew Morewood of the Hallowes, Dronfield –
and so the list goes on, surprisingly rapid changes in occupation
for such a substantial property. Even a century ago the But-
chers, a pair of bachelors, were experiencing trouble from
urbanites snatching their turnips and hedge-stakes. Harold
Armitage's comment that "farming near a large industrial
centre is not an experience that tends to philosophic calm" is
even more pertinent today and would be a colossal under-
statement were farmers still living at Lees Hall. As it is, the old
house and buildings have been completely levelled (as has
neighbouring Cockshutts Farm), and the remains of the valley
are to be developed as the Lees Hall Urban Fringe, a sort of
semi-wild area to contrast with the formality of Meersbrook
Park.

Armitage's description of Lees Hall just a century ago may

take some believing if one wanders there today – "always it seemed like a country Sunday afternoon." Not far across the stream now rise the tower blocks of the Gleadless Valley Estate, planned for seventeen thousand people, with houses from two to six storeys making the best use of the surprisingly steep site. This may well be an unusual place to live (attracting architects and town-planners from far and near), but it does nothing for the delights of the valley which it overlooks. Vandals have wrecked any old buildings and chopped at the ancient trees; rubbish lies in the once crystal stream, and Armitage's "atmosphere of peace and decorum" surrounding Lees Hall has gone like autumnal mist.

The name of the stream seems to have been derived from Anglo-Saxon words for 'a boundary', and until 1934 the Meersbrook formed the boundary between Derbyshire and Yorkshire; in fact, this was the age-old frontier between Mercia and Northumbria and between the more recent provinces of Canterbury and York. All the land to the south and west of the stream lay in Derbyshire, in the parish of Norton. In 1934 this large parish was transferred to the city of Sheffield.

The old turnpike road leading southwards from Sheffield to Chesterfield and London climbed out of the Sheaf Valley at Heeley and rounded the western side of Meersbrook Park and up towards Norton along what is now called Derbyshire Lane; then across Norton Park (now Graves Park and Sheffield's largest park), along Dyche Lane to Coal Aston and so down Green Lane to Dronfield. At some time it seems that an alternative route was made down Scarsdale Road from Derbyshire Lane and through Woodseats and up Meadowhead Hill where the main road runs today.

A last look back to Sheffield from the top of Meersbrook Park brings to my mind the recent description by R. C. Scriven of his native town. He recalls that Sheffield was in daylight at the beginning of this century "an eyesore more notorious even than the Black Country". Yes, our view of the city is far clearer than ever it could have been since the coming of serious, wholesale industry. But at night a lot of the magic is now missing. R. C. Scriven again:

When I was born in Sheffield it had a dramatic infernal beauty by

night. On all its hills the cones of blast furnaces were tilted at ran-
dom intervals and the lurid crimson glow of their fires glared like
the eyes of demons.

The smoking, reeking witch's cauldron of Edwardian Sheffield,
Bessemer's mistress, the honest tart with her sleeves rolled up, was
my Sheffield. Today it has some of the purest air in polluted England.

You can certainly appreciate that on a nice day in Meersbrook
Park, from somewhere near the Bishops' House; Sheffield
backed by its broad hills of the south Pennines, lovely gritstone
country.

Up and down Derbyshire Lane two centuries ago came daily
the donkeys carrying milk in pannier-churns from the farms of
Norton parish to the expanding population of the industrial
town beside the Rivers Sheaf and Don. One of these donkey-
driving lads became one of Britain's best-known and best-loved
artists, the finest of all sculptors.

When Harold Armitage's local history entitled *Chantrey Land*
(to which I have already referred above) was published in 1910,
that area of the north Derbyshire-West Riding border-country
which was the homeland of Sir Francis Chantrey appeared
rural still. But even so, the author lamented the advance of 'civi-
lization' crowding breathlessly from the Sheffield side and
threatening the peace and beauty that Chantrey knew so well.
He never lost the deep love for his native countryside and
revisited it often, even after he rose to international fame and
honour.

Most of Chantreyland lies in the parish of Norton, an
ancient Derbyshire village which was taken into the city of
Sheffield in 1934 and is now a southern suburb of that conurbation. Tower blocks of council flats, from their ridge-top sites
at Greenhill and Gleadless, peer across the wooded recesses of
the Moss Valley, which is really the heart of Chantrey country.
The little River Moss is fed by three headwater streams which
rise near Lightwood, Norton and Coal Aston respectively and
then flow eastwards to join the River Rother immediately east
of Eckington – a total distance of but five miles. The upper
basin of this small river, above the hamlet of Ford, is Chantreyland.

Norton village is the focal-point for all pilgrims seeking associations of this great artist.

The Chantreys had been a fairly well-to-do family, and some of them had been to university – one had been a rector – but their prosperity seems to have waned some little time before Francis was born in a small cottage at Jordanthorpe at seven o' clock in the morning of 7th April 1781. His father was a carpenter and small farmer. Armitage records that young Francis attended Norton village school "very irregularly, for no doubt there was much for him to do on the farm or in the workshop". From infancy he drew pictures and was allowed, every Saturday, to cover the stone floor of the kitchen with drawings before his mother washed it.

Francis began work as an apprentice to a Sheffield grocer but soon afterwards managed to transfer to the shop of Robert Ramsey, wood-carver and dealer in prints and plaster models, of High Street, Sheffield. He spent his spare time in modelling and drawing in a rented room in Hutton's Yard. Later he tried his fortunes in Dublin and Edinburgh, finally going to London in 1802, where he worked as a wood-carver. What really brought Chantrey to the public notice was his bust of Horne Tooke, exhibited at the Royal Academy in 1811, when the artist was almost thirty.

Today he is perhaps best known for his equestrian statues of George IV in Trafalgar Square and Windsor Castle, but Chantrey himself considered his finest works to be the figure of Lady Frederic Stanhope at Chevening and the bust of Sir Walter Scott at Abbotsford.

Armitage's book describes all of Chantreyland, and in considerable detail – names, places, people past and present. I consider it a classic of local history, four hundred pages of fascinating material illustrated with scores of evocative pen-and-ink sketches by the local artist Charles Ashmore; he is a master of adding just sufficient detail to create a freedom for the imagination to roam. Clouds and shadows cross some of his skies, others are blank; a hen scratches by an old wall, a mop-capped woman carries a bucket across a stackyard; rooks fly to tall trees.

In the remarkably hot summer of 1976 I remember going down into Owler Car Wood from the Coal Aston side, crossing the River Moss, then reduced to a barely perceptible trickle, and following the old bridle road northwards by Newfield Spring Wood. The August afternoon was hot and lifeless; no birds sang as I came across the shimmering stubblefields to find Hazelbarrow Farm, still standing amid open fields and looking, to quote Armitage, "down Dowie Lumb towards Ridgeway". What we see today is but a shadow of the former ancient hall, which was demolished about 1810. This was the home of the de Haselbarrows in the thirteenth century. The present farm-house was a modification of part of the lovely old hall, and some features of the latter remain in the garden. Most of the substantial farm buildings have survived, and a picturesque buttress at the north-east corner of the garden appears yet in place. Charles Ashmore's evocative line-drawings in *Chantrey Land* include a view of the Elizabethan gateway, leading from the rickyard where hens are seen scratching for spilt grain. I was delighted to find hens still at work in that old gateway.

One mile to the south-east of Hazelbarrow stands Povey Farm. This is a typical Elizabethan farmhouse, which, according to Armitage, lies in "one of the parts of Norton that have retained their rural character untouched by other influences". This remains true today, for one looks out southwards from Povey across the Moss Valley to the woods and fields about Troway and Sicklebrook. Francis Chantrey must have known this pastoral landscape well; he would recognize it still. From there I went on to Norton village (literally 'north farm', in relation to Dronfield a couple of miles to the south) and its several important mansions, the most significant of which is The Oakes, or Oakes-in-Norton. The name is taken from the great wealth of oak trees found in this area – Evelyn's 'Sylva' and Hunter's 'Hallamshire' refer to Sheffield's fine oaks – and gnarled specimens still dot the park here. The Morewood and Gill families lived here long ago, but it is the Bagshawes who have become synonymous with Oakes-in-Norton and who live here to this day.

The house was built in the seventeenth century but was completely remodelled in 1827, resulting in a plain, nine-bay, two-and-a-half-storey building complete with Tuscan porch. It is open to the public in summertime. The terrace on the south front of the house was designed by Chantrey for Sir William

Bagshawe, and the large urns there were a gift from the artist.

The beautiful iron gates, mentioned by Armitage as being "amongst the treasures of the Oakes", are still to be seen. They were made from metal obtained from Delves Wood on the estate and are thought to have been cast here.

School Lane bounds the western perimeter of Oakes Park, and here, until recently, stood the old school, rebuilt and enlarged in 1787. Chantrey attended this spasmodically, but Armitage mourned the fact that it was no longer the village school in 1910, serving as a private theatre in the grounds of Sir Nathaniel Creswick's home. A while ago the school was demolished, and suburban villas occupy the site. On the other side of School Lane, adjoining the main gates to The Oakes, I was pleased to see the old Post Office, which was illustrated on the frontispiece of *Chantrey Land*.

School Lane leads to Cinderhill Lane, and Jordanthorpe. The *Punch* artist Linley Sambourne was brought up in Jordanthorpe Hall by his Aunt Linley. My maternal grandfather spent his childhood here too, and how surprised he would be to find the old house serving as council flats. Across the drive stands the farm which was Chantrey's birthplace. In those days it was a small cottage, but when Chantrey became wealthy he had it enlarged for his mother, who lived there until her death in 1826. A special school has been built in front of this farmhouse — spoiling the outlook from it, but the structure remains much as it did after Chantrey had finished with it. Even the original window of the bedroom in which he was born can be seen facing towards the north-east.

The heart of Norton village lies a quarter of a mile to the north of Jordanthorpe, centred upon the parish church of St James. It is known that there was a church here when Robert FitzRanulph, lord of Norton and Alfreton, founded the abbey at Beauchief not far away because he bestowed it to that abbey, and, until the Dissolution, a regular canon of Beauchief officiated and resided here. In the chancel is a memorial tablet to Sir Francis Chantrey, the work of his former assistant James Heffernan, and in more recent times a full-length plaster cast of Chantrey by John Bell has been erected there.

After his sudden death at his London home in November 1841, Chantrey lay "in a gallery surrounded by the models of

his works". It is recorded that his old friend J. M. W. Turner
came the day after his death "but could not speak". He would
have a particular affection for Chantrey, knowing the latter's
homeland from those early forays with a pencil and sketchpad
when he was seeking his fortune and Chantrey was a boy of
twelve, long before their paths had crossed – though it is not
beyond the bounds of possibility that young Francis could have
seen the older artist at work at Meersbrook as he himself drove
the milk donkey down Derbyshire Lane from Jordanthorpe.

Chantrey had always intended to be buried in Norton
churchyard and had years before chosen the spot under the
south face of the tower. It took the undertaker and his team six
days to reach the village with the corpse, and the burial took
place in driving rain on the afternoon of 6th December. The
granite tomb is plain to the point of severity because Chantrey
disliked ornamentation for its own sake. The inscription is extremely deeply cut (he knew well enough the effects of weathering on shallow inscriptions and on soft stone).

Immediately to the west of the church stands Norton Hall,
which was for a long period the home of the Shores (who also
lived at Meersbrook House.) After 1850 it was owned by a succession of wealthy families and more recently served as a Sheffield hospital annexe. When the mansion was rebuilt in 1815,
Chantrey poured scorn on the new design and described it as a
"packing-box with windows in".

Upon the remains of Norton Green, close to the church,
stands the great obelisk of Cornish Cheeswring granite
designed by Philip Hardwick and erected in 1854 as a memorial
to Chantrey. Another tangible memorial is the Chantrey
Bequest to the Royal Academy. The artist left his fortune to his
wife, and upon her death in 1875 income from it was to be spent
on the most valuable works of sculpture and painting executed
by artists of any nationality who were resident in the United
Kingdom when the work was executed. The purchases of the
Chantrey Bequest are housed in the Tate Gallery.

Chantreyland remains remarkably intact, despite the red-
brick housing estates encroaching from the north and west,
plans for a sewerage works in Hazelbarrow's fields, and a by-
pass road through Oakes Park, near the south front of the
house. Standing on a quiet summer day in Lightwood Lane, or

in the woods above the Moss, we can appreciate Harold Armitage's sentiments all those years ago – Chantrey's name will never be forgotten in the region of "the church, the halls and the cottages that stand in the midst of Norton's quiet fields".

8

A Pattern of Fields

Fields form a major part of our landscape. Where the soil allows, the ingenuity of man has, down the centuries, imposed cultivation on heath and moor and marsh and woodland in fields of unlikely shape and form, of a thousand and one sizes and with a tremendous variety of names.

The first fields were open fields, created in the Middle Ages and usually numbering three to each village. If their form has passed into oblivion, their identity often lingers on in local place-names, as at Turlow Fields, near Hognaston, and Hatton Fields, near Hatton, both in south Derbyshire. The three great fields attached to a manor grew two cereal crops, and one-third of the acreage would lie fallow each year, to rest it and to control weeds and pests.

This was, of course, before the widespread use of the so-called 'fallow crops' such as turnips, swedes and potatoes. The coming of these useful plants meant that the farmer could cause the idle one-third of his land to become productive, for he could 'clean' the soil between the wider rows as the root crop matured. It meant also that he could at last supply freshly-grown vegetable matter to his over-wintering livestock and so reduce the formerly inevitable slaughter of the majority of his animals as winter set in.

Only at Laxton, in Nottinghamshire, can we see the three-field system still used today. And what a dramatic sight it is – the great West Field, Mill Field and South Field spread beneath the wide eastern sky to reflect the countryside of medieval England. Such farming systems were all well and good when the lord ruled his manor, but farms became independent and some land was broken up at an early date into individual acreages. Fences, hedges and walls began to spread across the land, chequer-board fashion or snake-like.

However, the break-up of the great fields accelerated considerably towards the close of the eighteenth century. Early enclosure was done by means of private Acts of Parliament but later by private agreement between individuals and finally in a fully organized way by Enclosure Awards.

Geoffrey Grigson has shown how the result of general enclosure of the land was "a revolution in way of life and in landscape". In the past villages were largely groups of farmhouses, from which the men went out to the great fields on most days of the year. After enclosure this pattern sometimes remained, and it is still possible to find villages or hamlets made up largely of farmhouses. Monyash upon the central limestone plateau of Derbyshire is a good example. But enclosure in some areas resulted in the farmers moving lock, stock and barrel to new houses, and buildings being erected on their portion of the original open fields, now enclosed by wall and hedge.

When enclosure came, as it did eventually to almost all the cultivable low ground of England, it took two main forms – the apparently haphazard, patchwork enclosure by walls and hedges and fences in an endless variety of shapes and areas, and the regular, usually rectangular enclosure of land. Why these two contrasting patterns, often in close proximity within one parish? The answer is not too difficult to find.

The haphazard form was the result of enclosure which came piecemeal, over an extended period of time, and which adhered to original boundaries of the great open fields and woodlands. The common shape of the plough-strips of the medieval open fields was a reverse-S, caused by the fact that an ox team of eight animals (four pairs) required considerable space in which to turn at the headland. By curving the furrows at each end of the field, the ploughman could get his team round in the shortest distance and with the least confusion. The hedges or stone walls often followed this curve and can be seen in many parts of Derbyshire. The finest example known to me is on the edge of the Holmesfield-Barlow parish boundary 950 feet above sea level, in the vicinity of the so-called Meek Fields, near Moorhall in the north of the county.

The complicated story of how the face of the countryside

was altered by the evolution from open to enclosed arable cultivation and pasturage during the last two centuries is a fascinating one, and nowhere can this story be better seen than in Derbyshire.

There is that finely curving field, almost 950 feet above sea level. For many years its narrow, graceful sweep has fascinated me, twisting tantalizingly over the horizon between the stone walls that enclose it. The field forms part of the Meek Fields, an elevated complex of land that is not very fertile, and so has earned this name.

But how did that particular field on the parish boundary come to be so long and narrow and curving? By coincidence Dr S. R. Eyre was born and brought up not two miles distant from it, and he, more than anyone else, has explained the significance of field patterns and shapes. He has shown why some areas of upland Derbyshire are composed of irregular and curving field shapes.

On the one hand there are districts where the fields are regular rectangles of various areas but uniform in outline and presenting a rather bleak pattern. Such enclosed land is best seen near Loades (above Holymoorside village to the west of Chesterfield) and adjoining the extensive and ill-drained moorland known as Leash Fen. They are relics either of the parliamentary enclosure awards of the early nineteenth century (which resulted in the break-up of the great open fields of the ancient three-field system of arable farming) or of the systematic enclosure of former rough moorland – intake land.

On the other hand we find large areas where the fields appear on first examination to be of completely haphazard form and of greatly varying area. Few of the boundaries, whether wall or hedge, are straight. These are fossilized field patterns, remnants of the plough-strips of the original open fields. Dr Eyre has shown that these great open fields were enclosed piecemeal, probably over a considerable period of time. Hence much of this enclosure pattern remains to show us the lines taken by the medieval cultivators.

What is remarkable to the careful observer is that most of the remaining ridge-and-furrow to be seen is curving, not straight as one would expect. And it has been shown that the form of the curve is invariably that of "an elongated and reversed letter S".

This is an exact description of the fascinating field that forms part of the Meek Fields. Now, because the medieval cultivators never left any written account of their techniques, we are left to conjecture.

At one time it was thought that the lands were gracefully curved to steady the flow-off of surface water and so prevent excessive erosion. But the plough-strips sometimes ran up and down a slope, sometimes across it. And why was the curve always in the form of a reversed-S when an S-shape would be equally effective as an anti-erosion device?

The answer would seem to lie at the end of another avenue. Several historians consider the reason was to facilitate a smooth and easy exit from the ploughing and, subsequently, a more satisfactory entry into the next furrow to be ploughed. The ploughman was faced with turning furrows on a narrow strip of land using a team of maybe eight oxen in four sets of pairs. It is known that almost all medieval ploughs had a fixed share and mouldboard on the right side of the implement – as in modern times – so that the soil was turned over to the right.

Before the widespread introduction of underground drainage by stone soughs and, more recently, by earthenware drainage-pipes or 'tiles', it was usual to plough the land in high ridges – sometimes five or six feet at their crests above the bottom of the furrows – to help drain the land. The only satisfactory way to plough round a high ridge was to work round it in a clockwise direction, bearing in mind the right-sided position of the share and mouldboard. With a leftward turn at the end of a run, the ploughman could keep the mouldboard firmly against the furrow slice, so helping to prevent it from dropping back into the furrow that had just been opened up.

With a team of eight oxen, one can well imagine a massive headland would be required for them to turn round. Such large headlands would not be practicable if the open-field system were to work satisfactorily, because the head of every strip would then have to be separated from its neighbour by a great area of unproductive ground.

Having turned his ox-team to the left, at right angles to the line of ploughing, the ploughman and his assistant could then manœuvre the animals and plough sharply round to the right (clockwise) so that it was comparatively easy to enter the fresh ground to be ploughed, entering at an angle less than ninety degrees to the headland. And so the reversed-S form was ideal for ploughing the field strips.

The serpentine field on the parish boundary seems to be a fossilized open-field strip. It is likely that the reversed-S shape of cultivation had become a thing of the past by the end of the sixteenth century, partly as a result of improved ox-breeding, which resulted in larger and stronger animals so that a smaller team was required to haul the plough. The development of conservation of winter 'keep' (largely hay) meant that towards the end of the Middle Ages the oxen began spring ploughing in better condition than formerly.

Both these improvements meant that the curving plough-strip became obsolete. The fields on either side of this particular field are not of reversed-S shape so it is quite likely that at the break-up of the open-field system this particular strip was retained as a headland or as a means of access to land on the far side. At a later date it would have been closed off from the adjoining land by the stone walls seen today.

In this particular case it would seem that this reverse-S strip retained its ancient shape as an access strip for, to this day, it gives communication to land which would otherwise be surrounded by land in other hands.

Then we come to the other form of enclosure, the regular, usually rectangular form. This is often best observed in hill country, at the present fringe of cultivation. Some of this is true 'intake' land – fields taken in from the moorland edge and slowly brought into cultivation or, at worst, turned into reasonable pasturage. Some of the intake fields are very large and the walls (being hill country) very rectangular in pattern. Again in Derbyshire, in the parish of Hayfield there is land called The Intakes; at Hazelbadge there is Intake Farm; at Bakewell and at Cromford there is Intake Lane, and just over the county boundary in north-east Cheshire there is that bleak hill-top area near Chisworth called Ludworth Intakes.

All these and many more originated as moorland taken in with the help of the 'graver's spade.' A team of such cultivators consisted usually of two men, the graver using the large 'graver's spade' and his mate (the putter-over) turning over the sods he cut. It was a slow and laborious job, but it won land that would otherwise have long remained unproductive; it also gave men work when work was in short supply. A great intake field at Mossylee, near Glossop, is known as 'the Duke of Norfolk's Garden' because it was cultivated by local mill-workers when there was no other employment. The Duke of Norfolk's agent gave them the task of breaking up the moorland and enclosing it with high, gritstone walls against the future encroachment of heather and bracken.

One of the finest examples of intake land in the north of England is that occupying the site of the former Holy Moor three miles west of Chesterfield. According to a document dated 1584 in the Portland Collection, the district was called Howley More, a name perhaps coming from the earlier Norse 'haugr' (a hill or height) and the Old English 'leah' (a wood or woodland clearing). Such a 'hill clearing' would be taken in for cultivation quite early, but the regular pattern of rectangular fields came at about the same time as the general enclosure of the open fields, between one and a half and two centuries ago.

Not far to the north of Holy Moor are similar fields in close proximity to the upland hamlet of Wadshelf, a cold place facing the eastern lowlands at the very edge of Eastmoor in north Derbyshire. From the environs of adjoining Wigley there is a very clear view of these rectilinear enclosures. And 'enclosures' is a word used advisedly, for this land was formerly the cultivated land of Wada, according to the Domesday Book, land divided into three great fields – North Field, Nether Field and Wheatcroft Field. At the very beginning of the last century several of the original strips had already been enclosed; nine strips around the northern and western fringe of the great North Field, and seven strips in the lower part of the Nether Field, among others. Then around 1830 the total area of these three open fields was enclosed, largely by stone walls surrounding rectangular portions.

A small area at the western side of the former Wheatcroft Field is known as the Stud Fold, and this supports the firmly established local belief that here, upon the top of the broad ridge, the Romans kept their horses. This old tradition brings us to the subject of field names.

Several large volumes could be written about the names of fields of even a limited region, their location and their derivation. Field names are an essential part – and a very fascinating one at that – of the rich heritage of the countryside of these islands.

Most of the names of fields date from relatively early times and tell us something of the land use and state of agricultural husbandry of the era. Some field names describe characteristics of the land enclosed and here are a few examples.

In the parish of Parwich are Bad Flatts, Baldstones and Froghole. The latter suggests that the land is wet and poorly drained whereas not so far away, in the parish of Brassington, there is a field known from at least 1620 onwards as 'Shining Cliff' – literally 'the smooth valley', describing the unbroken slope of dry land lying on limestone rocks. In the parish of Bradley there are some interesting names which suggest former friction and strife: take, for instance, Encroachment and Slang. As examples of self-explanatory names there are (in the same parish) Three-Cornered Piece, Top Croft, Six Acres and Ox Close. Then in every parish there are many field names with apparently mysterious names which take more understanding. In Bradley parish, near Ashbourne, there is a field called Poison Piece – probably land containing water much polluted by an element such as lead where livestock did not thrive or even died.

Actually there is a considerable list of uncomplimentary names which usually refer to the infertility of the land thereabouts. Cheat-all Patch, Clam Park, Hungry Bank and Urine Close, Vinegar Hill and Wilderness are some of these. Treacle Nook occurs where a field's top-soil is largely clay and ill-drained.

Another field in Bradley parish is Vols (Vole's) Croft, which illustrates the sense of humour of long-dead yeomen in naming tiny fields appropriately. In other parts we find 'Wren Park' occurring no less than thirty times within the county of Derbyshire alone, again used ironically to describe a small area of land. Likewise Hen Park in the parish of Brampton, and Mouse Park, Threepenny Piece, Million Roods and Napkin Piece elsewhere.

Field shapes often give rise to particular names. Some Derbyshire examples are Cleaver-shaped Half Acres, Boot Foot and Rump of Beef. Wry Neck and Teakettle Handlepiece seem especially apt and attractive. Then it was fashionable to name enclosures after distant places – for patriotic reasons or to impress the neighbours? In the parish of Ashover are North Britain and Carolina. Elsewhere may be found New York, Land's End and Jericho.

Fields forming parts of old charities abound throughout the county, and we find them in connection with names such as Sacred Fields and Charity Field. Lastly, there is the mysterious side of the story of field nomenclature: fields and enclosures having picturesque but puzzling names such as Blue Button, Gingerbread Piece, Save All, Hundred Year and Three Week. We may never know the real explanation for the many truly fanciful field names; but perhaps it is just as well for our rural heritage to retain some secret charms. On an Ordnance Survey map of 1840 showing the Melbourne district, for instance, is a field called Lapwing. The same place was in 1673 called Lapwinge flight. Why that delightful name? There is a mystery for some enterprising scholar to explain.

9

Winter at Hurley Grange

This is the story of a little-known valley on the eastern flanks of the Peak District in Derbyshire, a steep and wooded vale which slants up from the eastern lowlands near Chesterfield. Its upper end gives out onto the heather moors where, in winter, the snow often lies long and deep and the sheep have a hard time of it.

High up on a shelf above this upper vale lies a tiny hamlet which I shall call Hurley. The large farm is called Hurley Grange, and close by it is the cottage where a labourer and his family used to live. The cottage had been empty for fifteen years, and the sole occupants of Hurley Grange were a pair of ageing bachelor brothers who farmed the 170 acres around them.

I used to pay regular visits to the farm, and one occasion stands out in retrospect as particularly memorable. It was a bitterly cold January evening, a black night sky punctuated by the brightest of frosty stars as I ploughed through the crusty snow towards a faint outline of naked sycamores. No yellow light was visible as I approached Hurley Grange, no lamplight shining from the living-room or the swing of a lantern from the yard. No sound came across the frosted landscape.

The old brothers at Hurley had lived here alone ever since their mother died twenty years before, and the work involved in running the place had gradually become too much for them. The land was becoming overgrown, the buildings decaying and the workforce slower and stiffer. The elder brother, Albert, had a completely stiff leg – it had been so for fifty years – and Fred, the younger, a bad back which had developed alongside a general slowing down and lack of energy. Even the regular, day-to-day duties (such as feeding the cattle and mucking out the cowsheds) were becoming too much for them.

As I came up to Hurley on that winter's evening a faint glimmer became visible at last as I climbed a gate into the yard. The flicker of a paraffin lamp now shone through the dusty living-room window, outlining geraniums festooned within by spiders' webs. A knock on the door, a distant "Come in, who-ever yer are!" from somewhere beyond, and I walked down the black, dank corridor to the fire—and lamp-light—where the aged brothers usually sat, leaning towards the leaping flames with outstretched hands the better to keep warm. A pile of cats dreamed atop the inky Yorkshire range, adjacent to a steaming kettle.

Hurley Grange was a farm which had not moved with the times. There was no electricity or gas, not even a reliable water supply. A large tank collected rainwater from the farmhouse roof, and this was used for the household; in dry summer weather this was soon exhausted, and thereafter one or other of the brothers fetched water in milk churns from a brook a quarter of a mile away. The animals relied on a trickle from a cast-iron pipe supplying a stone trough. In winter they had to be turned out from their sheds twice a day, as in days of old. During severe frosts the provision of water for the animals took up many hours of tedious work each day.

Albert spent ever more time confined to the house after his seventieth birthday, complaining of lack of vigour and appetite. He continued to do what housework he could, and I sometimes arrived to find him dusty with flour after a spate of dumpling-making. A grubby newspaper covered the table as he thumped and rolled a greyish lump of pastry with hands blackened from recent attention to the fire. His stiff leg gave greater pain and immobility as time went by, and he spent several days at a time in bed.

That dark night in January I arrived to find Fred dozing on the sofa by a dying fire. He was surrounded by the usual huddle of cats, one wheezing asthmatically. Eventually he turned and announced that Albert had "taken to his bed last week" and that he was finding it a "big job" to climb the stairs with refreshment on account of his severe rupture and painful back. At that moment there came a loud thumping upon the ceiling overhead.

"Go up and see what he wants," Fred instructed, and I

passed out of the flickering lamplight into a black passage where progress was slowed by altercations with damp clothing hanging from pegs on one side. This was no good; I returned to the light of the living-room and borrowed a hurricane lamp and started out again.

An old rope was draped down the spiral stairs, no doubt used by Albert to haul himself up. The yellow light from my lamp illuminated the dank and mildewed walls of the upper passage, at the end of which I could see faint light issuing through a door partly ajar.

"Come on up here, lad – aren't I glad to see thee!" came a faint voice. The sight which met my eyes was something from a Victorian novel. A shambles of neglect lit by pale candlelight smacked of the utter poverty of a Dickensian dockland garret in a Brontëland setting.

Albert lay on an iron bedstead in one corner of the large room; he was propped up on several ticking-covered pillows and covered by filthy blankets and a piece of ragged carpet. On his head was the usual cap, and I could make out that he was clad in shirt and waistcoat. His face was black with grime. A few sacks were tucked around him to keep out some of the icy draught. On the rickety chair beside the bed was an old bean tin which apparently did service as a chamber-pot. The candlelight threw a huge and dancing shadow of the old man on to the grimy wall. On another wall a mouldy print of a cavalry charge by Lady Butler was festooned with ancient cobwebs.

"Aren't I glad to see thee!" he repeated, "He'll starve me, you know – not a bite to eat all day and only a cold cup o' tea since daybreak." Clearly the housekeeper below was not doing his best. I went downstairs and soon returned with food and a hot drink.

This procedure continued for several weeks. Sometimes Albert managed to descend and keep warm by the fire, but he became worried that Fred was not coping with the livestock, and one night when I arrived he had taken to his bed again and asked me to go and investigate why the cattle were calling loudly from their stalls.

Downstairs sleepy Fred admitted that he had not been outside that day, and there was no water in the yard trough. With a failing torch I began carrying buckets of water to the thirsty animals, then, directed by Fred, took around buckets of corn and armfuls of hay. By midnight, with the stars bright in the black sky, the work was done, and Albert was able to rest easily in his sooty bedroom. Unfortunately Fred now relied on my assistance nightly, and no farm work seemed to be done until after the last light of those short days had long since faded. As Albert pointed out, "The trouble with 'im is that he's gotten out of his stride – he doesn't stir till afternoon, then it's falling dusk and he's done nowt outside!"

Things came to such a pass that Albert was getting sustenance only when I went up the valley to the farm. Likewise, the animals were being watered and properly fed only when I had struggled with buckets and flickering lamp in the icy blast whistling straight off the moor.

I often took hot food up to Hurley Grange at this time, though it was barely warm when the eager brothers ate it. After one such chilly meal Albert (who had managed to struggle downstairs for a few hours) decided he would attempt an ascent to the black bedroom. "Tha'll 'ave to use all they strength, tha' knows," he directed to Fred, "I'm no mountain goat so tha'll 'ave to shuv me up them stairs from behind; and you'll 'ave to light the route," he nodded to me. The expedition set out down the long, dark corridor. Half an hour later we had hauled on the stairway rope and staggered along the upper corridor and Albert was finally seated on his bed. I went downstairs to fetch a thermos flask of tea which would sustain him in the coming hours. As I came back up the stairs again, Fred was being instructed loudly to help Albert undress.

"Get me boot off that foot first! Damned fool! Now – get me trousers over me stiff leg. Oh dear, tha're a clown! Tha' knows I canna' bend that leg! Stand back, then, Useless – I'll do it me sen," the exasperated Albert was shouting. At last, though, we were able to leave the bedroom where the invalid lay with his huge, dancing shadow upon the murky wall.

Fred took a further quarter of an hour to descend the stair and reach the friendly light of the living-room. Then I went out into the blackness to attend to the lowing cattle in their sheds.

One night when I went up to the bedroom, Albert asked me if I could hear his little pals. I listened and heard a scurrying of tiny feet and much squeaking. "They're me mice. There's a nest of 'em in this mattress. When I lie still they come out and take crumbs from me 'and. The only trouble is they wake me when they run o'er me face in t'night. Anyhow, they're company.''

He recalled how one night recently he had put his hand down the bed to stroke the cat lying next to him beneath the blankets. Only when it climbed up across his chest and leaped onto the windowsill did he discover it was a large brown rat. "They're no friends o' mine. If one pokes its head out from behind that dressing-table I throw this empty aspirin bottle but I usually miss!" he laughed.

Those dark, winter days have passed. Fred and Albert now live in retirement in a village at the edge of the moor, and Hurley Grange lies empty and forlorn where the Pennine wind whistles through the lonely sycamores.

The valley below is a quiet place; in some weathers it is silent to the point of desperation. Birds do sometimes sing but only spasmodically. Throughout all that long and lonely valley below Hurley one can wander and rarely see another living soul. I suppose it is wonderful to know of countryside near home where there is always peace, but the valley does have a sort of neglected air, like a valley cleared by Noah before the Deluge began.

The soils here are not particularly fertile, and the slopes are quite steep. Lower down the valley there are three reservoirs, and so no one lives down near the feeder streams – not that they ever did, but people from the hamlets on the ridges enclosing the valley used to work and relax here, far from the bustle of Chesterfield and from any tarmac roadway. As in so many small communities of the past, communities which worked in their own parish for the most part and died there in the end, there were many individualists, characters in their own right who were a constant source of amusement or frightful fascination for children and of gossip and conjecture for adults.

There lived in one of the hamlets on the ridge not so far from Hurley Grange a very stout woman – she must have weighed twenty stones though no one in the place owned a pair of scales, and no light-hearted cajoling would entice her on to a neighbouring farmer's corn-scales when she helped with the threshing. Despite her huge size she worked hard in the fields, helping farmers on a part-time basis when there were potatoes to pick, turnips to pull and the winter threshing in some dusty stack-yard. Some said that this hard work caused the colossal appe-tite which maintained her prodigious volume; others considered it was due to the malfunctioning of her "inward parts". Whatever the cause, 'Old Sal', as she was known to everyone, lost not an ounce, summer or winter.

As she got older and work out of doors got less, she actually grew larger and finally became so gross that she rarely left her cottage. There were stories of her hoarding habits, of a bed-room so full of newspapers that the door could not be opened any more.

"I don't know where she gets all that paper from; and what her mother would say if she could see the place now I just don't know!" was the theme of most conversations about Old Sal in her last years.

With the draining away of the true native inhabitants of the district and the typical influx of wealthy urbanites, Old Sal's cottage became isolated by expensive stone walls and inter-woven wooden fencing. Her neighbours were strangers who had no time for a dirty old woman who rather spoilt the tone of the place. In earlier years an old woman was known to everyone, and her life-long acquaintances would help her, children would run errands and younger women clean the windows or take round a hot meal in severe weather.

One bleak winter day an old man from the neighbouring vil-lage came by Old Sal's cottage and thought he would see how she was coping after the recent snowfall. There was no reply to his knocking, and the curtains were drawn at the window so he went round to the rear of the place but still got no reply. At the bottom of the narrow garden the earth closet stood like a sentry-box draped in its blanket of snow. There were no footprints be-tween the back door and the privy, but he went down to it and pushed open the door.

Old Sal lay stiff as a board on a soggy cushion. A candle had burned itself out in the tiny recess in the wall, and there was an empty bowl and spoon beside the body.

Later it was discovered that the old woman had been living in her earth closet for almost six months because her cottage was filled with newspapers and cardboard boxes – literally crammed with folded newspapers, every room and the cellar. Old Sal had actually been forced out through the back door by the inevitably diminishing space as she folded the daily paper and placed it on the pile which had outgrown even her vast bulk. People who knew her recalled comments about saving the paper "in case it came in handy sometime". Old Sal had indeed developed an obsession which eventually destroyed her in winter's icy hold.

Further down the ridge stands another village, more sheltered than Hurley Grange or that where the fat woman lived. There is a red brick school here, a typical Victorian village school with separate doors for boys and girls. It is not so many years ago that local children entered this school at the age of five and completed their formal education here a decade later. Theirs was a world of school where little ever changed – the same staff for year after year, playmates were classmates, the caretaker lived close at hand (and had done since the beginning of time for all the children knew). It was a secure world, and there were none of the traumas associated with a change of school for few of these children 'passed the scholarship' to the grammar school in Chesterfield.

This particular school had a peripatetic music teacher, a severe middle-aged lady with wispy grey hair, who came once a week to teach the brightest of the older pupils the rudiments of playing a variety of instruments. Musical appreciation was not a strength shared by all her scholars. One day, for instance, a boy reached home to tell the family that there had been a rumpus in the music lesson; when the music teacher arrived that morning, she went to the cupboard where the instruments were stored.

"She were ever so mad because someone had bitten the end off the 'cello," he explained.

"Which end?" asked his aunt.

"The end you blow through," was the reply. Further questioning revealed the instrument to be an oboe.

No one ever owned up to the deed, and music lessons did not last much longer at that school. Needless to relate, the boy never aspired to a career in music.

10

Corner, Knob and High-Stepper

There is a field not so very far from my home which is filled with memories. Whenever I go that way and look to that hillside field above the narrow, wooded valley floor, I remember days long since gone; hot days in summer when the scent of hay was in the air, wet days when grey clouds scudded in from the high moor to the west, and frosty days when all the world was pure and white and very still.

The field in question stands above the farmstead where I worked. It faces out across the little valley towards the south and so receives all the warmth of the sun and is well sheltered along its western boundary by tall trees which border a steep and fast-flowing brook descending to the bottom of the main valley. All the farm traffic between the farm buildings and the hillside fields behind must pass through this large Home Field. It has been down to permanent pasture throughout living memory.

Many years ago the farmer of the previous generation expanded his poultry interests by placing several large wooden huts around the field. The breeding flocks of fowls inhabited these assorted buildings and the field – in bright sunlight the hundreds of russet Rhode Island Red hens and arrogant, agile Black Leghorn cockerels made an arresting picture.

The first house was placed near the centre of the field and, because of its sloping roof, was called 'the Lean-To'. Another was put on an elevated mound near the top of the field and was known as 'the Knob'. Its neighbour was a smaller, taller house entered by a step and hence called 'the High-Stepper'. The cote adjacent to a gap in the nearby hedge came to be known down the years as 'the Gap', and the long house standing parallel to the top of the stackyard wall was 'the Cote Across'. The wooden coach-house of the gentleman's residence next to the farm was purchased and moved at some date after the arrival of the Lean-To and, because it occupied the top corner of the field beneath aged hollies, was 'the Corner Cote'.

The labour involved in looking after the hundreds of breeding birds was considerable, of course. Carrying water, for instance, was often a tiresome business. Adjacent to most of the houses were large tanks, filled in wet weather by rainwater from the roof guttering, so that the day-to-day watering was simply a matter of filling buckets and then filling the drinking-cans inside the cotes. The problems came in hot, dry weather and during severe frost when it was necessary to cart water in ten-gallon churns in a cart converted to be towed by the tractor. First I would back the cart alongside the stone trough in the farmyard and laboriously fill the five or six churns with a bucket. Then I drove the load to the tanks alongside the different cotes. Finally came the tricky job of lifting the full churns on to the top of the cart-side and tipping the contents into the tank. Usually I got well soaked by the splashing caused by the cascade; sometimes the wet churn would slip on the icy top of the tank and fall to the ground, the water emptying as it went. If conditions were very severe, I might take half an hour smashing the ice from the tank before emptying the churns; so often such weather resulted in the freshly-carted water being frozen before the afternoon visit to fill the individual drinking-cans inside each house.

I recall the extra labour of maintaining paraffin lamps placed under the water-cans in those poultry houses during long spells of frost. If all else failed, there was no alternative but to carry buckets of water from the yard around the field.

Feeding the hundreds of birds was a time-consuming task, too, but was less unpleasant than carting water in winter. Every few days we filled the wooden hoppers inside the poultry houses with pellets. This entailed splitting hundredweight sacks so that they were more easily handled in the field. If only one or two houses required pellets, I would carry the split bags on the back of the tractor, but this sometimes resulted in spilling pellets across the grass. This was not too serious, though, as the nearest hens always quickly found the scattered food and cleared it up.

The flocks had wheat night and morning, strewn from a bucket when the eggs were collected. What a fine picture those massed birds made at feeding time, and what patterns one could make across the field by scattering the grain in curving lines. When the sun shone on the backs of the masses of pecking Rhode Island Reds, the proud Black Leghorn cockerels standing by, the scene was truly beautiful.

As the grain bucket emptied, so the egg bucket filled. Trap nesting was carried out in a couple of cotes nearest the farmyard – the Dairy and Second Cotes – and this necessitated collecting the eggs five or six times daily, lifting the birds from the trap nests, reading the number on the leg ring and re-setting the traps. In this way the best laying birds could be selected from records made over a lengthy period of time.

All this round-the-field tramping was far more onerous in the mud and rain of winter. Carrying full buckets of eggs in the teeth of a westerly gale and pulling one's feet from the squelchy ooze on a January afternoon as the light failed had the bonus of a respite as each cote was reached, offering welcome shelter within as the eggs were collected and grain thrown down upon the straw. At such times of bad weather the hens were not let out, and once each door had been shut behind one, the poultry work was finished for that day.

At all other times the pop-holes used by the birds had to be fastened at nightfall, when all had retired to their perches. This was particularly tiresome when dusk descended later in the evening, though I had usually gone home and was not involved. On many occasions my employer had an anxious return from an evening outing, hoping to reach the pop-holes before Reynard came on his nightly prowl.

Now and again a hen would for some reason stay out, perching optimistically in a holly tree or hawthorn hedge. Such birds were rarely seen again; often, though, we would discover a handful of bloody feathers or a leg cast in the long grass. What was feared most of all was the nightmare of a fox entering a cote by a broken window or by pulling netting from a gap in the boards. This happened more than once in my experience. The result was brutal murder. Scores of birds had their heads snipped from their bodies and strewn about the hut, where utter confusion reigned. Foxes will kill as many birds as possible in such an attack, apparently for the sheer joy of the exercise (as cat with mouse) and rarely carry off more than a couple of carcases for consumption in a safer place.

The low roofs of some of the cotes were a hazard when moving about inside. I remember several skull-cracking, knee-knocking encounters with the low roof timbers of the Lean-to Cote, all the more annoying because one was so familiar with the place and normally aware of the offending beams.

Those same roofs gave extra work in times of high winds. The early morning rounds of the field after a rough night brought reports of a lifting roof or broken window. Later in the day we took materials and repaired the damage.

A weekly job entailed the removing of droppings which had accumulated on the boards under the rows of perches, where the birds spent the night and part of wet or snowy days, when they were confined to cote. Fortunately for me the farmer's wife's aged uncle took care of this work when he was well enough. Uncle Ben was stone-deaf and very lame. He would creep around the field, leaning on a draw hoe carried in one hand and dragging in the other a sack of empty sacks and a dust pan. Meticulously he deftly scraped the droppings onto the dust pan and deposited them into the sack at his feet. After dragging the filled sacks outside, Uncle Ben slowly made painful progress to the next cote.

It was my job to go round the field later and empty the filthy sacks into the cart or muck spreader. After heavy rain, when the sacks were soaked and sticky, or after frost, when the muck was frozen solid inside, it was miserable work. Only the carting of water in icy weather and the hand-cutting of kale and lifting of mangolds in similar conditions were comparably unpleasant to me.

One cleaning-out task in the poultry houses which I didn't escape was the removal of the soiled floor-covering of wood shavings and straw. In some cotes this work was particularly tiresome as the door was at one end and the mucking-out entailed a walk of many yards with each forkful of bedding; the Knob and the Cote Across stand out in memory as the worst in that respect.

In hot, dry weather Uncle Ben could be seen applying the annual coat of preserving creosote to the external walls of each house. Despite a knotted handkerchief held down with an old cap, he finished each such day with a well-stained face which gave the impression of a rich sun-tan which must have been very sore. With long-handled brush and bucket, an apron of sacking and that handkerchief around his face, he looked for all the world like a desert-weary sheik whose camel had trotted off.

With the passage of the years the free-range system of keeping breeding hens lost ground to more labour-efficient systems. New deep-litter houses appeared at the edge of the Home Field, just beyond the stackyard wall. The Dairy, Knob, Corner Cote, High-Stepper and others fell into disuse, though the Knob and Gap were used until recent times to house breeding turkeys. The High-Stepper was destroyed by fire in August 1978, and the Cote Across fell down and was then dismantled.

Uncle Ben is no longer to be seen moving slowly from cote to cote dragging his bagful of sacks; he has gone now to his long rest in the hill-top churchyard just visible from the Home Field. The empty hen cotes can still be picked out from the surrounding high ground; their dark profiles bring back memories of busy days as they decay gently in the shelter of the tall trees which break the west wind.

Another memory comes back vividly in the context of those fields just a little higher up the slope above the Home Field.

It was one of those remarkably fine October days which occur now and again and remain in the memory. A bright sun shone warmly across the slanting fields, and the air stood still between every hedgerow. Away to the west the Big Wood reared upon its hillock, patchy yellow and green where the first larch needles were falling close beside the evergreen pines. Across the sleeping valley the tall chimneys of the Tudor mansion rose from the buildings which they dominated; closer at hand the dyke trickled towards the valley floor, glinting between the brambles and the willowherb bank.

Wood pigeons were murmuring from the fox covert, and the rooks criss-crossed the sky. All the world was at peace that day as we picked the potatoes in the Great Lamb Croft. That morning we had done remarkably well in picking a dozen rows, and the break for a drink at eleven-thirty had been particularly attractive. So we had the break for dinner. Now, we had picked three afternoon rows and were awaiting the return of the tractor to spin out the next one.

Robert lay on an empty sack and threw stones for the good dog Laddie; Dick was emptying the last bucket of potatoes while David held open a sack for him. In those few quiet minutes it seemed that all the world stood still and that it was impossible for winter to come.

Soon the tractor had come down the field, and we were up on our feet. David put the spinner in gear, and out came the potatoes, like new-born piglets, onto the warm dry soil. Our backs were bent again.

For the rest of the day we picked the crop and relaxed on the empty sacks when the tractor was late coming down the field. It was a pleasant surprise to have emptied the last bucket as David held the sack open and to see the others farther up the field still hard at work. Tea came in a cardboard box late on that mellow October afternoon, and how good the buttered scone tasted, how welcome the hot tea.

As the sun went down beyond the Big Wood, we picked up the last row of the day and began to load the full sacks on to the trailer. When that was done, we all climbed on top of the sacks and went down slowly through the dusky fields to the sleeping farm.

The next morning was very different. A dense grey fog wrapped the countryside, and a late start was made. It was quite a job to find the gate in to the potato field and not easy to measure out accurately the length of row each picker should be allocated. The picking then began.

The fog lifted a little towards noon, but it was still not possible to see more than two pickers along the row. What a miserable day it was – no birds sang and the trickling brook could not be heard through the blanket of fog.

On the previous day we had thrown some of the smallest potatoes at each other, and now some of these potent missiles whirred again and we ducked in the hope of avoiding their invisible flight. Suddenly, from somewhere far up the field, we all heard another whirring, and I, for one, thought another small potato had been thrown in our direction.

But the noise grew louder, and it continued. It was coming from a greater distance and the din quickly filled the air about us. The whirring became a deafening roar which seemed to come at us in the greyness from every direction. There was no escape, and I stood awaiting the fate which now seemed inevitable. In those few seconds of explosive noise and rushing air there was time to see those nearest up the row raising their arms as they crouched. There was a sudden draught and the fog was blown aside; a great thud and we were blown off our feet into the unpicked potato rows. We were showered by small stones and particles of soil and potatoes. The potatoes flew at us, bruising us cruelly as they came.

Then there was silence and the fog was wrapped about everything as before. There were shouts from far up the field and we picked ourselves up from the debris of soil and stones and potatoes. What small cuts we had were caused by flying stones, and we were soon searching across the field for the cause of the bombardment.

Robert came to the edge of a sudden downward slope of steep soil and stopped David from going headlong down into the abyss in his haste. The crater – for such it proved to be – must have been twenty feet deep and forty feet in diameter. We could just see the far side in the curling mist. But from the bottom of the hole steam was rising to displace the fog above.

The explosion, the crater and the thickening mist brought to an end the day's potato-picking, and we were all keen to know what had caused such excitement. Conjecture led to the exercise of some fantastic imaginations – a bomb had fallen accidentally; someone wished to put an end to David; someone hoped that I would leave my motorcycle to them; then we wondered if Marples had thrown a large stone at us and missed.

Early next day we came down through the wood beneath a heavy sky of cloud. The wind now blowing out of the south-west had cleared the fog during the hours of darkness. We vaulted over the last fence and gazed down the potato field to a chaotic heap of soil, stones and sacks. Soon we were looking down into the crater again. Almost buried by soil and stones at the bottom of the hole was a dark, marble-like object which we slowly exposed by scraping back the soil. It was rock and very hard. After half an hour we managed to lever the rock out of its bed with a broken hedge-stake. It was a lump two feet long, one foot wide and maybe one foot deep. It was of great density for it proved impossible to haul it out of the crater until William arrived with his tractor.

There was no doubt about it now; we had experienced the landing of a meteorite, and an uncomfortably close landing it had been.

"I'm glad it wasn't the size of a tractor," observed Robert "or they'd have been picking us up and putting us in bags instead of the potatoes!"

11

More Threshing Days

It is a refreshing experience to see, hear and smell a working traction-engine, even if it now has to be in the artificial surroundings of a steam rally. The quiet dignity of the external combustion engine, as exemplified by the traction-engine and the steam-roller, represents the very summit of man's combined mechanical and aesthetic ingenuity.

The forerunner of the true traction-engine used by threshing contractors was the stationary steam-engine. It was hauled by horses from farm to farm and provided the power for driving the threshing-drum and straw-trusser or straw-chopper. Then came the true traction-engines which propelled themselves, hauled loads and drove threshing machinery. They were the most versatile and powerful vehicles that man had devised for road work. What a sight it must have been to see a Fowler or a Robey road-locomotive hauling as many as five laden drays of grain along a lane. Upwards of fifty tons were hauled by such engines. It is little wonder that they ousted the heavy horse for the really heavy work on farm and road.

The steam-roller was the last representative of this wonderful family of giants to do regular day-to-day service. It is not so many years ago that steam-rollers were common on the road, and until the last ten years or so there were many old rollers standing idle and rusting in council yards throughout the country. Those that were not broken up for scrap are in private hands and fully restored.

How well I remember the hot, summer days when tar-spraying was done, when dust mingled with the heady scent of hot tar, and steam drifted with the soft, black smoke from the roller as it chuff-chuffed to and fro along a newly-laid strip of road surface. In front of the roller were the men who heated the

tar and spread it with a pipe; they were followed by men casting
gravel on it with hot shovels. They were a frightening bunch to
me, dirty and tarred and grim – none more so than the steam-
roller driver. He was always in the shadows and the steam beneath the roller roof and rarely emerged into the sunlight. We
did, though, get a proper glimpse of him at the end of the day.
The council yard, where his roller and caravan were based
while working in our district, stood close to my house in a
Derbyshire High Street. Every tea-time after school in the tar-
spraying season I would wait for the distant sound of the roller
as it approached the council yard.

When it had rumbled and puffed into the yard and stood
quietly steaming for the night, the driver would climb down
and go up the steps to his high, wooden caravan. Through the
open half-door could be heard the clatter of pots and saucepans
as he made his evening meal; the roller-man's caravan has
always seemed a romantic sort of place.

A rather different type of machine made at one time in quantity was the very versatile convertible-engine. The front roller
could be readily removed and replaced by normal front wheels
for road haulage work. Such a convertible is Mr H. Gurnhill's
1923 Marshall which is often seen at steam rallies in perfectly
restored condition after spending its whole working life with
Lindsey County Council. An interesting fact about this particular Marshall convertible is that it was last used as a steam
roller when the roundabout at Caenby Corner, Lincolnshire
was made.

The steam-roller, steam road-locomotive, showman's
tractor, cultivating-engines and steam-wagons are all fascinating, but for most countrymen the general purpose traction-
engine, as used by threshing contractors, is of the greatest interest. The well-preserved specimens include E. A. Twigger's
1936 Fowler No. 21647 'Little John'. This was one of the last
traction-engines manufactured and was exhibited at the Cork
Agricultural Show in 1936. For twenty-six years thereafter it
was in general use in Ireland, finally being re-imported into this
country in 1962. The deep maroon of its boiler and the shining
brasswork set off this fine twelve-tonner, glinting in the summer
sunlight at rallies each year.

But it was at the heart of winter that the threshing contractor

The grave of Sir Francis Chantrey in Norton churchyard, with Norton Hall behind. (Chapter 7)

The S-shaped field in the Meek Fields, Moorhall, winter. (Chapter 8)

The old barn at
Hurley Grange,
north Derbyshire.
(Chapter 9)

The bachelor
brothers at Hurley
Grange, summer
1976. (Chapter 9)

The High-Stepper (left) and the Knob. 'Many years ago the farmer
of the previous generation expanded his poultry interests by placing
several large wooden huts around the field.' (Chapter 10)

Carting water to the lean-to in frosty weather. 'Sometimes the wet
churn would slip on the icy top of the tank and fall to the ground.'
(Chapter 10)

The late Henry Helliwell thatching a corn stack at Horsleygate in 1971. (Chapter 11)

Threshing at Horsleygate, 1971. (Chapter 11)

The mouth of Alport Dale from the Roman road near Upper Ashop Farm, Hope Woodlands. (Chapter 13)

Looking across Ladybower Reservoir to the site of Derwent village from the war memorial. Derwent Edge behind. (Chapter 13)

The impounding wall of Derwent Reservoir in stormy weather,
December 1974 (Chapter 13).

Piers of the railway bridge built for
the construction of Howden Reservoir
early this century, revealed here in
drought conditions, 1976 (Chapter
13).

Summer in Wildboar Clough
northern perimeter of Bleakl
(Chapter 13).

Crowden Great Brook and Laddow Rocks from the upper part of
Wildboar Clough, looking across Longdendale (Chapter 13).

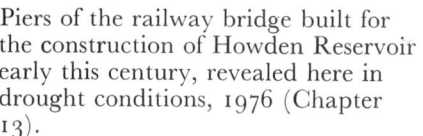

Old cottages at Brightholmlee, high above the mouth of Ewden Dale (Chapter 14).

Upper Ewden Dale from the south-east, showing Raynor House Farm, Broomhead Reservoir and the Broomhead Moors (Chapter 14).

The remains of Broomhead Hall before demolition (Chapter 14).

In the quarry at Little Matlock about 1902. Reuben Dearden, the author's maternal grandfather, standing at left foreground (Chapter 14).

was at his busiest, moving from farm to farm with thresh-ing-drum, baler and trusser. My old friend Mr Ned Morgan of Ashgate, Chesterfield recalls many remarkable experiences during his life as a north Derbyshire thresherman. Even in the days before the last war, the Board of Trade carried out regular inspections of traction-engine boilers with a view to main-taining safety standards. It so happened that the Morgan threshing outfit was parked at a little farm near Barlow Com-monside, where they had been working. On the day in question Ned Morgan was helping one of his brothers – also a threshing contractor – on a different farm when the boiler inspector arrived. He was told where the engine could be found and set off to make his inspection. Now the owners of this little place were two bachelor brothers and their sister. They were noted in the district for their eccentricity, but Ned Morgan recalls that they were utterly trustworthy, upright folk. The elderly sister, called Margaretta, always paid for the work done at the end of each day's thresh, wishing "to owe no man anything".

When the inspector arrived at the farm, old Margaretta took him to the covered-up traction engine and stayed with him while he carried out his scrutiny, to make sure that he was genuine. When he had finished, he replaced the tarpaulin and tied it down.

"Tie that again," Margaretta snapped, "just as tha' fun' it!" The man did as he was told and went away to report to Ned Morgan. He told him that he thought Ned had some peculiar customers on his threshing round and that he had never before been told what to do while carrying out a boiler inspection.

Then there were the spells of bad weather which often delayed the work. On one occasion Ned and his men had taken the outfit to a farm at Edensor, on the Chatsworth estate, and set it up in readiness for threshing next day when a snowstorm developed. They had a long cycle-ride home over the high ground of Eastmoor in the dark and only just managed to get through the drifts in the driving snowfall.

At Longstone one winter the weather deteriorated when they arrived at a farm for a couple of days' threshing. The drum, Ned remembers, had to be set up some distance from the corn stacks because of the steepness of the stackyard. This meant that a large team of workers was required as the sheaves had to be carried from stack to drum. At the same time it meant that the straw (which was chopped for horse and cattle feed) could be handled by one man because of the closeness of the storage building.

The weather continued wet and the threshermen stayed at the farm, hoping for an improvement each day. One evening they went to the local public house, and the old farmer with whom they were staying had far too much to drink, so much so that he had to be helped home. On getting to the farm, he began to have severe cramp attacks, leaping to his feet in agony. Ned Morgan laughs as he recalls that the very next day the weather was fine and they started to thresh early. There was no sign of the old farmer until ten o'clock, when he appeared at the kitchen door looking far from well.

"Yes, yo beggars," he groaned, "It's all they fault for getting me drunk last neet!"

At Wardlow Mires on one occasion the weather was so bad that after the first day's thresh they gave up any hope of continuing and went home until the following week.

A very different memory concerns the early part of World War II. Ned Morgan had driven his threshing outfit to Owler Lee Farm, near Holmesfield, and because there was the risk of an air-raid he left the traction-engine in the middle of the yard so that if any corn stacks should catch fire, the engine would be safe. He pushed his bicycle up through the wood and from the top of the hill looked back over Sheffield, where all seemed quiet. At Holmesfield he called to see his cousins at their farm, where Oswald forecast that "We're going to have a real neet!" Soon Ned was on his way again, and some way down Millthorpe Lane he heard the distant wail of the air-raid siren. He stopped and dismounted – should he go back and move the threshing-drum from the side of the corn stack where it had been set up in readiness for the next day's work? He decided not to and cycled homewards, taking to the fields to by-pass Chesterfield some miles farther on.

Down the grassy curves of Brockwell Lane he came to Holme Farm and there, as he crossed the darkened fields, the German bombers thundered overhead. At Loundsley Green an old man was standing in the blackness by his door and said, as Ned went by, "Good night, Mr Morgan. We're in for a hell of a neet!"

How he recognized Ned Morgan in the darkness was not certain, though few people would have been coming home at that late hour.

That night Sheffield had its most devastating air-raid. Next morning they threshed in the cold winter sunlight at Owler Lee Farm as if nothing unusual had happened, though a pall of black smoke curled over Sheffield in the valley below them. Ned Morgan remembers his relief at seeing quite clearly in the sunshine his brother threshing that day at another farm on a hillside across the valley at Dore.

Some of the farms where the Morgan threshing outfit went were the homes of generous people; other farms had happy or sad or silent folk. Some farmers were miserly or their wives parsimonious; in fact, his customers were a typical cross-section of the rural population of those times. "There's nowt so queer as folk," and Ned was quick to notice the remarkable traits of the families with whom he came into contact.

One place which he visited for many years had a farmer's wife who was keenly aware of the passage of time and counted minutes of work lost as money well and truly thrown away. "There were no intervals on that farm, not with her watching from behind the curtains!" he said recently. One of her tricks (witnessed by a keen-eyed youth looking through the kitchen window one day when the corn was being threshed) was to pour the tea for the mid-morning break from a great height into the assembled mugs, so cooling it down so that there would be no delay while the men drank it. Not content with that, she was seen to bend down and blow on each steaming mug in turn before the daughter was despatched with it into the stack yard. The daughter, as keen as her mother where time and money were involved, always made a concerted effort to race up the ladder with the tea for the band-cutter and his mate so that they would not waste seconds in climbing down to ground level and then, maybe, sit down on sheaves or bales out of the biting wind. Such penny-pinching antics always amused those who knew the family and those who helped on that farm on threshing days.

The threshing outfit of olden times almost always had a selection of unique characters who 'followed', that is, they sought temporary work on farms when the thresher went there.

One such character was known to be rather simple, son of an old established farming family, physically not excessively strong. Some said his mental faculties matched his muscle-power. One cold winter's day Ned Morgan completed a day's thresh at a hillside farm above Cordwell Valley and, as most of the tidying up of the stackyard had been done, this fellow made his way to the house where he knew tea was being prepared for everyone. He went into the kitchen and, without being asked, sat down at the large table where a plate of twenty buttered tea-cakes awaited the threshermen. While the farmer's wife and sister mashed the tea, he helped himself to a teacake and another, and another – until the women saw (half annoyed at his gluttony, half amused at his unthinking bad manners) the plate empty. They took it away and filled it again, taking the precaution of waiting until the other men came in before replacing it on the table.

When Ned Morgan took his new 7 hp single-cylinder Burrell traction-engine to thresh at Bowling Green Farm, high above Haddon Hall, permission was obtained from the Duke of Rutland to cross the River Wye by the narrow bridge carrying the private drive to Haddon Hall. The width between the bridge parapets was seven feet ten inches and the traction engine was seven feet eight inches wide so they got over without a moment's hesitation. Though the farmer was waiting at the bottom of the steep drive up to the farm with his heavy horses, Ned had every confidence in the new Burrell engine and sailed up with drum and straw-chopper.

Most of the maintenance in those days was strictly do-it-yourself, though major overhauls, such as a boiler rebuild, were usually done by a skilled craftsman sent by the manufacturer. Ned Morgan remembers fetching six boiler tubes from the Chesterfield Tube Company for repairs to the Burrell engine at Newgate, Barlow. The tubes were 5 feet $8\frac{1}{2}$ inches long, and he fastened three to either side of the cross-bar on his bicycle. On another occasion he fetched a thirteen-feet-long steam-pipe from Vicar Lane, Chesterfield and transported it in the same way.

"I didn't attempt riding the bike until I was well out of town, though," Ned recalls, "If I'd wobbled with that thirteen-feet pipe I'd have injured somebody."

A boiler engineer who had been repairing a traction-engine at Newgate, and had been helped by the young Ned, asked him if he would care to go to the next job with him, in the south, as he was so useful, but Ned's father refused to let him go because there was so much work to do at home. "You never know," he laughs when telling the tale, "if I'd gone I would probably never have come home to work again – and my father knew it!"

12

East to West Across Peakland

The subject of this chapter is a recent ninety-mile ramble which took us from the heart of Sherwood Forest, near the Major Oak, to the heights of eastern Cheshire. We took most of four days in fine July weather, but if one pressed on and sought out less detail along the way the route could be done in three days.

For the sake of completeness I will mention briefly the first day's walk, as far as the edge of the Drone Valley above Dronfield, though it traversed country outside the scope of this book.

At 10.30 am on a bright Sunday morning we set off along the wide ride leading straight as an arrow shaft between dark conifers, northwards from close to Villa Real. We were at the heart of ancient Sherwood, a sea of conifers isolating the massive oaks which are the true natives of the district. In a few miles we had passed close to the Major Oak and entered the true country of the Dukeries, by Thoresby, Clumber Park and the vast estate of Welbeck. And so, in 13¼ miles, we came under gathering cloud to Welbeck Bar and passed into Derbyshire.

Up through dreary Hodthorpe with its southerly view of colliery and cornfields which sweep away towards the ocean of woodland edging Welbeck Park. Then the red brick of Whitwell; actually only eastern Whitwell is like that, for at the centre of the settlement there is a dramatic change in character. Ancient Whitwell is as lovely as any village of Derbyshire, built largely of mellow magnesian limestone and pan tiles and in complete contrast to the urbane eastern half. Whitwell means 'the clear spring' or 'the pure stream' – tributary of the Millwood Brook. Two buildings impress themselves on the observer. The first is the old parish church of St Lawrence, notable for its Norman tower and the chancel erected between 1300 and 1350. The other building – close to the church on its northern side – is Whitwell Manor House overlooking the graveyard. It gives the impression of great size and complex design, possessing fine mullioned windows looking to the west.

And it was towards the west that we continued, out across Whitwell Common as the clouds began to break and sunlight spilt all about us as we went. On Bondhay Common the grass and corn were illumined brightly, bringing out all the gorgeous colours of high summer and backed by the dark horizon of Whitwell Wood.

Barlborough Hall and its park lay ahead as we gained Pebley Cottages beside the disused colliery. Crossing the wide, grassy sweep of the ancient park we looked fruitlessly for the herd of deer, which were not there, and gasped at the northern vista of sunlit lake and the far lands of corn and coal towards Kiveton and Todwick. We came up towards the great avenue of limes and glimpsed the lemon front of the sixteenth-century Hall, its many windows glinting in the late sun. A short sprint across the drive brought us to that sudden and exhilarating westwards revelation of a free, wide land, for we were at the crest of the magnesian limestone escarpment. Our belvedere revealed the great, blue spaces of the southern Pennines.

"Oh, dear!" gasped John.

"I had never thought of that," I replied, "And crossing isn't going to be safe."

We had heard an unpleasant roar for some time as we advanced across Barlborough Park, and now came the only miserable part of the day – of our four days. We had suddenly come into sight of the M1 Motorway, and what a sad prospect in all that golden light and freedom of westward space and far, blue hills. All that noise and those poor occupants of fast-moving vehicles, imprisoned where they sat.

By pure chance we came into sight of the Motorway where a farm track went beneath it, and so it was only a matter of minutes before we emerged onto the wide fields that fall down by Spinkhill. At 6 pm we sat in the tea-time sunshine on the wall bordering the Catholic Church of the Immaculate Conception, the dark stone seeming unusual after all those limestone miles. The present church was erected in 1846, but there was a place of worship here from about 1600. The copper dome of Mount St Mary's College shone green beyond the tall spire, and a west wind refreshed us as we contemplated the last miles of this lovely day. Now, we had anticipated a proper rest and a bite to eat at about this hour; we had looked forward to it for some time as our last stop had been four hours ago, when we had lunched under silver birches at the edge of Welbeck Park. We stopped only a few minutes at the Church of the Immaculate Conception above those golden corn lands which sweep down towards the Rother Valley.

The crossing of Whitwell Common had made us foot-sore, and it was a change to go downhill the short distance to Renishaw and then we were ascending by the wooded way through the parkland of Renishaw Hall. The turrets and chimneystacks of this famous house of romantic and literary association came into view over the grassy slope as we crossed above the Great Lake, making westwards. How refreshing to tired legs and sore feet was that melancholy view down to the lake, framed on the far shore by a drift of pink thrown up by rosebay willowherb.

At 7 pm we began the upward advance through fields to the Handleys. My memories of this three-hundred-feet ascent from the Rother Valley to the hill-top Handleys are shot through with beauty revealed and annoyance at our slow progress. Behind us the magnesian limestone was fully lit by the western sun, and Barlborough Hall's glorious turrets shone white from above the ancient surround of great trees. Spinkhill's green dome and dark spire, Bolsover's yellow castle and, distantly to the southward, rose Hardwick sending us on our way across those endless barley fields. Our progress seemed leisurely in the extreme, and I was convinced that it was only a matter of minutes before we would be surprised and accused of trespass. As we gained the lane climbing this eastern slope from Staveley to Nether Handley, the great, characteristic bulk of Belle Vue Farm came close into view – one of the bulkiest and trimmest farmhouses one could imagine. And there, waiting for us in her paddock before the farm, was Belle Vue Pearl, who had just gained high honours at the Royal Show – a truly wonderful Shire mare and in the true tradition of the Widdowson family of Belle Vue upon its hill-top at Nether Handley.

It was after 8 pm as we wound our way over the fields to West Handley. Lenticular clouds veiled the lowering sun and gave the impression of a close-approaching sundown. We still had to go several miles to our bivouac above the Barlow Vale. John was valiantly fighting great blisters and dragged doggedly behind Tom and me as we gained the lane at West Handley. A farmer was putting a large white sow to bed in a field hut as John came by, and he offered us shelter for the night, but John was determined to make that bivouac at all costs, and on we went. By the darkening shadows of Stubbing Wood we drifted along the trackway to Hundall.

Here was another sudden vista revealed below, far towards the head of the Drone Valley with haze hiding much of homeland Dronfield. Twenty-seven miles lay behind us, and there were only three miles more ahead to our woodland haven above Monk Wood, where we knew food, water and sleeping-bags were waiting under the bracken.

John and Tom took liquid refreshment at the hill-perch of Hundall, and then we made quickly down through Unstone village and across the railway line by the old station footbridge. It was 9.15 pm, and in failing light on that warm July evening we climbed the cornfields towards Bull Close. We could just make out the profile of Unstone Manor House across the slope towards the railway, as we could the field poppies dotting the wheat as we ascended.

Corn and root crops were crossed as we gained the sunset brow beneath Ouzelbank. The western sky was bright pink, and wide banners of still cloud reflected the glory of that high summer sundown. Under the trees we went, by Bull Close Farm where the lights were already lit, and out then above the edge of Monk Wood. Far below the evening valley was still, and lights were winking from Barlow and Commonside and from as far away as Cutthorpe as we came to the dark trees at the edge of the golf course.

It was very dark as we wound on through the low hollies, then out into the vague light of the golf course itself – across the final tee and so to our bivouac.

Just below our meadow site stood Less Common Farm, and in the very last light we located our cache of food, sleeping-bag and pressure-stove. Dark clouds were blowing on the lightest wind as we prepared our late meal at ten o'clock. There was a sudden crashing of undergrowth at the wood's edge not ten yards distant – a fox or badger which had sauntered towards us unaware of our presence until the last moment. Darkness shrouded the tall trees which cut out the westerward prospect, and we settled in our sleeping-bags for the short night.

With my high-altitude sleeping-bag-cover, intended for bivouacking in the Himalaya, I felt secure against anything which the elements might produce. I peered out into the night at 3 am, and there, quite low in the south, the full moon shone from a clear sky, framed by one of the three rowans which over-hung our camp site. The first, grey light of a cloudy dawn at 3.45 am brought heavy spots of rain, and I curled lower in my bag.

It was obvious that the high-altitude bag-cover in which I had placed so much confidence was suitable for turning only the slightest dew! At 6.50 am the rain stopped, and we got up beneath a rain-threatening sky. Wood pigeons and thrushes were calling as we breakfasted; by 7.30 am a sunny sky was showing, and we set off all smiling through School Wood and so by Cowley Bottom. By now the clouds had cleared away towards the east, and we went along the ridge by Hills Farm in brilliance, out across the head of the Gosforth Valley and so up ancient Oxclose Lane to Dronfield Woodhouse.

The footpath took us over the fields by Birchin Lee and there, with a bright sun and wonderful white cumulus clouds adrift, the great hollow of the upper Sheaf Valley lay before us. This was one of the finest moments of the walk, a truly opal morning. Soon we would have covered the short distance to the little brook which is the Sheaf, the brook which is the county bound-ary between Derbyshire and South Yorkshire.

For the rest of that lovely day we went northwards through South Yorkshire by Totley, Dore, Ringinglow and Rivelin. Over the high ground of Bradfield Moors and by Bradfield we reached the earthwork of the Bar Dyke and still, a dozen miles away to the south-east, the water tower at Norton and the more remote mast on Glasshouse Common were clearly visible. At 6.15 pm we reached our cache of food in the deep bracken above the Ewden Beck. By 7.45 pm we were off again in an attempt to gain as much ground as possible before nightfall – in particular to leave the tenacious midges and the rhododendrons and bracken far behind. The jungle hindered progress, and as we went the clouds now building up on the western horizon of

Upper Commons were getting denser and darker.

We bivouacked behind a tumbled gritstone wall, the better to keep dry from the scudding showers which came and went throughout the night. The next morning we experienced the most tedious and arduous walking of the journey, amid the cotton grass of Sugden Top where the curlews called in the stiff breeze and pipits flitted from tuft to tuft. By 10.45 am, however, we had gained ancient Cut Gate which sweeps over the grit-stone heights between Penistone and the coal-measure country to Derwent Dale. On the watershed we met the first rambler of the journey – an old man with blowing white hair – and took breath as we admired the westward prospect between Win Hill and Holme Moss. It was a landscape of brightest green, of bil-berry and bracken dotted with the pink of early heather. And so down to the Derwent beneath the lonely Horse Stone, down to the river and across the county boundary into Derbyshire once more.

The afternoon hours of head-wind and sunshine took us along the summit ridge of Bleaklow. We found two men floun-dering in the chocolate wastes between Bleaklow Hill and Bleaklow Head. They had set out from Edale that morning *en route* for the Scottish border but had already lost their Pennine Way. Near to exhaustion and caked in wet peat, we led them back to Bleaklow Head and set them on the undefined way towards Torside Clough and Longdendale.

Then we were off across the quagmire which interrupts the plateau between Bleaklow Head and the Higher Shelf Stones. All that windy afternoon we enjoyed spectacular views to the north and west beneath broken islands of whitest cumulus, away towards Lancashire's Pendle Hill and the nearby Holme Moss television mast. From our belvedere the blue, grey and white plumes of south Lancashire were cut by sunbeams; it was a land of promise indeed.

A quick run down the steep nine-hundred-feet slopes at the head of the clough drained by the Shelf Brook is remembered for the hot sunlight and the tanning wind as we went. Soon we were overtaking a hedgehog on the track which is the Roman road connecting Glossop and Brough – Doctor's Gate – and at 6 pm we passed Mossy Lee Farm. Now it was evening, and as we swung round to the south of Glossop on the lane by Moorfield and Gnat Hole, the profile of the church tower on Warhill and the dark outline of Cown Edge Rocks stood out in dramatic silhouette.

For three further miles we went to the south, along the Hayfield road. Then at 9 pm we came to the gnat-filled wood on the eastern slope of Lantern Pike. We cooked our meal with the little summit far above our heads as the mackerel sky reflected the pink glow of the western sun, as it had done two nights earlier. There was not a breath of wind, and we went to sleep as the last light bled from the sky behind our hill.

Once again a light drizzle fell at dawn on the next morning. Tom was up at 5.30 am, and we had a welcome mug of tea in our sleeping-bags. Soon the clouds were thinning, and long before we gained the top of Lantern Pike, the sun was out. Another beautiful day had begun.

We had now travelled more than seventy-two miles, and this would be our final day. I wished that it would go on indefinitely in these wonderful conditions. From this 1,177-feet-high vantage-point we could see the radio telescope at Jodrell Bank out on the Cheshire Plain; behind us the massive bulk of Kinder Scout lay impressively, topped by a gathering of dark cloud.

Down now to the sporadic conurbation which fills the floor of the Sett Valley – by Birch Vale, Pleasant View, Low Leighton and Newtown – then up a sunken lane onto the slopes of Black Hill.

By Kettleshulme and Windgather Youth Hostel and Cats Tor we reached Shining Tor at 2.30 pm and saw our goal – Shutlingsloe – dominating the trough of Wildboarclough. To the south we were able to make out the blue profiles of the Clee Hills, the Wrekin and the long line of the Denbigh Moors. So we drew close to Shutlingsloe, lit now from the west, where the grey hill sheep graze. Our ninety miles were done, and overhead was as fine a sky of fair weather cumulus as I think I have ever seen.

13

Three Bleaklow Valleys

Time and time again I find myself writing about the high grit-stone massif of Bleaklow, between the Woodhead and Snake roads. Much more extensive than neighbouring Kinder Scout and but a few feet less elevated, it offers much greater scope for rambling of the exploratory kind. The rock scenery is perhaps less generally dramatic than that of Kinder Scout, but its broad shoulders and deep and secret valleys make enchanting approach-ways to the ultimate heights.

In this chapter I have selected three such valleys, two of them true dales, which will give a good idea of the scope for enjoyment in some of the wildest country in the south Pennines.

During the latter part of the last century several large towns cast interested glances into the longest and most sinuous of Peakland's gritstone dales. Corporations responsible for providing reliable sources of pure water saw the assets of the beautiful upper Derwent Dale. This valley was cut out of relatively impervious gritstone and had steep slopes and a small human population. Dams thrown across its width would form large reserves of water which would then flow, aided by gravity, south towards Derby, Nottingham and Leicester. Sheffield lay but nine miles distant over the high moors to the east.

The Derwent Valley Water Act of 1899 enabled the first instalment of work to begin, involving the construction of two large masonry dams – Howden and Derwent – between 1901 and 1916. The Derwent Valley Water Act of 1920 authorized the building of the much larger Ladybower Reservoir lower down the dale. This contains 6,310 million gallons to be used mainly as compensation water for the River Derwent. Construction of Ladybower Reservoir began in 1935 and continued through the Second World War.

The flooding of the upper dale by Howden and Derwent Reservoirs, in the early years of the century, resulted in the inundation of thirteen of the lovely old farms which nestled in sheltered corners where tributary streams joined the Derwent. There was ancient Ronksley Farm beside Lynch Clough, close to the present head of the dale's road. In the Hope Parish Easter Roll for 1658, the Barber family were recorded as being resident there. Westend Farm stood near the confluence of the Westend River with the Derwent half a mile south of Ronksley. It served as a rest-house for travellers using the Glossop–Penistone packhorse track.

Ladybower Reservoir began to fill with water in March 1943. One arm of the new lake flooded the lower Ashop Valley, and the other filled Derwent Dale almost as far as the great impounding wall of Derwent Reservoir. Near the branching of these two arms of the new reservoir stood the village of Ashopton, which vanished under the rising water at a relatively early stage. A mile and a half up Derwent Dale was the picturesque village of Derwent, where a medieval packhorse bridge crossed the river close to the parish church and Derwent Hall.

The earliest authentic records relating to Derwent refer to the founding of an abbey grange by the Canons of Welbeck Abbey, Nottinghamshire, towards the end of the twelfth century. It was established on what is now the eastern bank of Howden Reservoir and remained an important outlying farm in the possession of the Premonstratensian order for three and a half centuries. After the Dissolution, in the sixteenth century, Derwent came to the Cavendish family and later still to the well-known local family of Balguy, which traced its pedigree back to the reign of Edward I.

In 1672 Henry Balguy erected the fine Hall close to the point where the monks had built the packhorse bridge over the Derwent. They were followed by the Newdigates, who sold the estate to the Howards, Dukes of Norfolk, in 1886. The eastern slope of Derwent Dale rises to the craggy crest of Derwent Edge, which undulates for over six miles from south to north and attains almost eighteen hundred feet in several places. The Howards used Derwent Hall as a shooting-lodge, and people still living in the vicinity remember the large shooting parties which came there each autumn before the Second World War.

In 1932 the Hall was opened by the Prince of Wales as a hostel of the YHA, and, at the end of that decade, it was dismantled as Ladybower Reservoir was being built. The attractive stone gateposts, topped with Tudor-style balls, were removed to the entrance to Woodthorpe Hall, near Holmesfield, a dozen miles away, near the eastern edge of the Peak District National Park. (See chapter 5.)

The packhorse bridge was also taken down, and each stone was numbered before being stored in a nearby barn. In 1959 the bridge was carefully re-erected at Slippery Stones, four miles upstream of its original site. It carries the Glossop-Penistone track over the river and is still much used by ramblers. Appropriately, it serves as a memorial to John Derry (1854–1937), a pioneer rambler and author of the first edition of *Across the Derbyshire Moors* (published in 1904).

Four chapels were established by the Premonstratensians in this wild situation: one adjoined the actual Abbey Grange three miles above Derwent; a second stood near the packhorse bridge in the village; a third was situated across the dale; and the last was built at a greater distance overlooking the Woodlands Valley. Following the Dissolution, the chapels fell into decay, though the one in the village, dedicated to St James, was served periodically by a curate. It was replaced about 1757 by what J. Charles Cox described as an "ugly little building". Just 110 years later, "this mean edifice, which had neither antiquity nor beauty to recommend it," was demolished and replaced by the last church.

As the waters rose ever closer towards the village, the interior of the church was stripped. The doors of the main entrance were taken to replace those at the parish church of Old Brampton, near Chesterfield. The war memorial was removed to a site beside the new, high-level road across the dale. At the end of the Second World War it was a miserable sight to look eastwards from the roadside war memorial. The tower of the church rose out of the water, isolated from the higher dwellings which were not to succumb. In the following years Derwent became a popular place with visitors, and after long spells of dry weather it was possible to cross the cracked bed of the reservoir to explore the ruins. Before anyone could become trapped or injured, the tower of the church was blown up.

During dry summers the water in each reservoir is reduced, and sometimes a few of the remains of Derwent village and some of the ancient isolated farms are revealed. In the dry summer of 1955 the old bridge across the former course of the Derwent stood high and dry in the bed of Derwent Reservoir, and on several subsequent occasions the remains of parts of Derwent village have become visible again. A heap of stones then marks the site of the church, and the drive to the Hall winds down by the Mill Brook, a tributary of the Derwent which drains this section of Derwent Edge. A water-mill formerly stood beside this brook, a reminder of the farming activities of the Premonstratensian monks who were resident here in the Middle Ages.

One of the major problems facing the Derwent Valley Water Board before a start could be made on the Howden and Derwent reservoirs was finding the most suitable source of gritstone for the dams and other masonry works. A final choice was made at Bole Hill, up on the high ground due north of Nether Padley some ten miles from the construction site. Here outcropped the coarse, quartzose gritstone known as Rivelin Grit, and here, as elsewhere where it comes to the surface, it is characterized by a rosy-pink colouration.

The top workings of the quarries reached to a thousand feet above sea level and six hundred feet above the Midland Railway line between Sheffield and Manchester just west of Totley Tunnel and close to Grindleford Station. It was estimated when work began at the very beginning of the century that there were 2,400,000 tons of sound Rivelin gritstone suitable for building at the site. The quarry expanded to cover an area of fifty-two acres and employed about six hundred men.

A great asset of the site was that, by constructing linking railways and an inclined cableway down to the Midland Railway line, it was possible to transport the stone for $3\frac{1}{2}$ miles on that route, up the Derwent Valley to Bamford. From Bamford the Derwent Valley Water Board built its own railway up the dale past Ashopton village (now flooded beneath Ladybower Reservoir) to the site of Howden Reservoir impounding wall near Marebottom Farm. The massive piers carrying this line across the mouth of Ouzelden Clough on the western bank of Derwent Reservoir are revealed in drought conditions and give a small indication of the huge cost of construction at Howden and Derwent, estimated in 1905 as being between six and seven million pounds when completed.

From the main line near Grindleford Station the Water Board built a double line on the flat which connected with a double-line incline cableway with a gradient of one in three and 750 feet long. This steep incline can still be seen. Above that a zigzag railway with a gradient of one in twenty-five ran up to the topmost quarry faces. About six thousand tons of building stone was produced here each week and sent on its devious ten-mile journey. It is interesting to note that the only work let out by contract here was that of dressing the face stones, those which lie today on the surface of the impounding walls and their towers.

Blocks of gritstone weighing from twenty to thirty tons were split from the face and brought by cranes down to the foot of the quarry face where the rough ends were knocked off and then the squared-up block lifted again to the banker (a piece of ground near each working face) where a man with a rock pick and a level squared up the joints and beds at right angles to the face of the block. This left a minimum of projecting stone for the mason to remove with his punch.

The mason and his assistant, the scappler, were paid nine shillings (forty-five pence) per superficial yard of the face measurement. Stones with a content less than twelve cubic feet were broken up and sent to the stone-crushers for use in the concrete. The finished blocks average fourteen cubic feet per ton, and during the twenty-seven month period between June 1903 and September 1905 the quantities sent from Grindleford to the construction site were 168,849 tons of rubble, 133,751 tons of displacers (reinforcing lumps of irregular shape to go into concrete) and 32,200 tons of dressed stone.

One problem at the Grindleford quarries was providing a satisfactory water supply. It was estimated that about twelve thousand gallons were needed on each working day of ten hours. Now the nearest adequate supply was a stream in a ravine 360 feet below the top working faces of the quarry. A hydraulic ram was fitted which could lift sixteen thousand gallons in twenty-four hours to a height of 350 feet. This water was pumped in tanks with a capacity of 35,000 gallons, and pipes carried it to the machinery and workshops where it was required. Breakages and leaks seem to have been a constant problem here, and, lecturing to the Society of Engineers on 4th December 1905, Benjamin L. Bradley explained that "tanks on wagon wheels are kept filled and are taken by locomotive to the place where the supply from the pipes is cut off." There were endless problems here at the quarry and ten miles away up Derwent Dale.

That well-known upland dale where so much water is stored cuts deep into the eastern flanks of Bleaklow. Another dale, smaller and sinuous and fortunately less well known to the general population, is that drained by the River Alport.

Travellers using the A57 between Sheffield and Manchester – the famous Snake road – are likely to miss seeing the mouth of Alport Dale as they cross it by Alport Bridge. Such oversight is due to the large trees which overhang the road, the river and the bridge.

To get a really good view of the lower dale, one should take the old trackway which leaves the Snake road at Alport Bridge, crosses the River Ashop by a ford and swings up the slope of Blackley Hey, at the north-eastern corner of the Kinder Scout plateau. This old trackway is actually a Roman road, connecting the fort of Anavio in the Hope Valley with the fort of Melandra, near Glossop. Looking back to the north a quarter of a mile from Alport Bridge, the broad mouth of Alport Dale is revealed. Steep and grassy slopes rear eight hundred feet as high, smooth sentinels of this fine valley.

Deciduous trees crowd beside the twisting course of the River Alport, and the dale swings away to the ever wilder heights of heather and peaty wastes. In the middle distance, looking from along the Roman road, plantations of conifers can be seen as punctuation marks on the far slopes, before the dale turns to the left and out of sight two miles above Alport Bridge. High on the right slope a rugged area of exposed rock can be made out. This feature is Alport Castles and is best seen at close quarters.

To explore this little-known Derbyshire dale of the gritstone plateau country one must, of course, walk. A track twists up to Alport hamlet from the Snake road at Heybridge Farm, but this must be used only as a public footpath.

The stone barns which dot the lower pastures of the Ashop

and Alport troughs are typical of the north country, with great doorways for the quick entry of loads of hay in this high rainfall district. Adjoining are shippons and calf-pens for wintering cattle. Such a barn is passed to the left of the track a quarter of a mile above the Snake road, and in a further three-quarters of a mile the remote hamlet of Alport is reached.

The name Alport is derived from Old English for 'old town' or fortification. The earliest known reference is in the Forest Proceedings of 1285. The tiny settlement now consists of two former cottages and Alport Castles Farm. The track curves round to the right to avoid a large barn and so enters the yard of the farm. This barn is the place where the historic Lovefeast takes place on the first Sunday every July.

With the authority of the infamous Act of Uniformity of 1662 many clergymen were ousted from their livings on 'Black Bartholomew Day' in the same year. Some of them made for the safety of this remote dale. Here they assembled "to worship God according to the dictates of their own consciences". In the eighteenth century John Wesley is said to have preached in the same barn while travelling between Lancashire and Yorkshire.

It was natural, then, that the early Wesleyans should establish their annual Lovefeast at this romantic spot, a ceremony which includes the singing of hymns and the partaking of plum loaf and water. No longer is the Lovefeast attended by a great crowd, many of which had walked miles across the hills; the few still participating now arrive at the Snake road by car.

The two cottages facing the Lovefeast barn now form a police adventure centre. Alport Castles Farm is still inhabited, though the land is tenanted by farmers near the Snake road. A path drops to the River Alport behind the farm. By following the river downstream a short distance, a footbridge can be used to cross to the eastern slope of the dale. High up on this flank, six hundred feet above the river and dominating this section of the dale, is the rugged scar of Alport Castles, Britain's largest landslip.

The path climbs up the steep, grassy slope eastwards for half a mile to the crest of Birchinlee Pasture at sixteen hundred feet above sea level and then down to the mouth of the River Westend, where it enters Howden Reservoir in popular Derwent Dale.

Near the top of the rise to Birchinlee Pasture is the huge landslip. The Rough Rock Group of millstone grit which forms the surface layers of the plateau-top here comprises a bed of hard sandstone (the Rough Rock) overlying a thick shale series which is comparatively soft. Constant weathering of the underlying shales has resulted in undermining and the collapse of the harder sandstone above, best seen in the east face of Mam Tor at the head of the Hope Valley five miles distant. Here at Alport Castles a great wedge of the plateau has broken away from the face behind and very slowly fallen out towards Alport Dale. As it has moved out and downwards over the centuries, a huge 'bow wave' of earth has formed in front of it. It is the largest landslip in these islands, and the late Professor W. H. Pearsall has stated that "there is no better example in Britain of the instability of mountain structures."

One can scramble to the top of the Tower, the top of the break-away block, and look at the extensive face of millstone grit acting as a backdrop for the sweep of Alport Dale as it winds northwards towards the heart of Bleaklow.

From the foot of Alport Castles a path can be followed to the north, a route which contours at about fourteen hundred feet above the narrowing dale. Eventually, where the last conifer plantation ends on this side, a good path develops. The scarred western slope a mile above Alport hamlet is called Grindlesgrain Tor, conspicuous from our path. It is in this vicinity that the last rowans are passed, in a side valley called Glethering Clough where dippers and ring ousel may be seen in summer. In May and June the call of the cuckoo is commonplace in the dale.

Out of sight from the path just below Glethering Clough is a small waterfall, where the Alport plunges into a secret pool beneath a rowan. Waterfalls are not common in the Peak District, and this is the lowermost of three which enhance this dale. The path winds for half a mile above Glethering Clough, and then the other two falls appear in quick succession at fourteen hundred feet above sea level. The uppermost is the finest, and after heavy rainfall on Bleaklow it is a dramatic sight.

The situation is a lonely one, just below the level of the exposed gritstone plateau. In the shelter below these falls were found the bodies of Scouts who had succumbed to exhaustion during the Four Inns Walk some years ago – after the spring weather had suddenly deteriorated. The remoteness of this dale-head is emphasized when it is recalled that the bodies were not located for a considerable time, despite a well-organized search over a wide area.

A mile above the waterfalls, and a hundred feet higher vertically, the sides of the dale open out to a broad basin. Here is the confluence of the Alport and its main tributary the Hern Brook. This place is called 'Grains in the Water', an ancient name evolved from the Old Norse '*grein*' (literally 'a fork of a river'). The broad basin is called 'the Swamp'. In summer the moor-grasses and bilberry bring colour, and it can be a sun-trap on a still, bright day; then the only sounds are the calls of curlews, dunlins and rock pipits, and the trickle of the Alport.

Less than a mile to the north of Grains in the Water is Alport Head, where the little river is born under the peaty crest of Bleaklow Hill, more than two thousand feet above sea level. This wide wilderness of Bleaklow is Britain's only true desert, often a dark waste of chocolate peat beneath gale-driven mist. A mile to the west is Bleaklow Head (2,060 feet), where the Pennine Way comes over from the head of the Snake Pass *en route* for Longdendale.

There are two Wildboar Cloughs in the southern Pennines, one a beautiful dale drained by the Clough Brook which is a tributary of the Dane, west of Buxton; the other is a steep and rugged gritstone ravine which cuts deeply into the northern flank of Bleaklow high above Longdendale. The latter Wildboar Clough is the third valley of this chapter.

Of the nine major cloughs or steep valleys which carry streams down the northern side of Bleaklow to the River Etherow in Longdendale, it is the third one from the west, Wildboar Clough, which is the most rocky and perhaps the most fascinating. Working eastwards from Glossop, there is little Ogden Clough, broad and mighty Torside Clough which is the main pedestrian thoroughfare as it carries the Pennine Way between Bleaklow Head (2,060 feet) and the Youth Hostel at Crowden. Most ramblers, therefore, miss Wildboar Clough, which comes next, almost a mile to the east of Torside Clough.

From Torside Clough there is an easy and pleasant traverse below Long Gutter Edge above Torside Reservoir. The lower

part of the clough, when first seen, does not suggest a particularly dramatic ravine, but once the watercourse comes clearly
into view the rocky gritstone walls are revealed.

The clough runs in a north-westerly direction, draining
Shining Clough Moss on the northern sides of the gentle Bleaklow watershed. Due to this aspect successful photography is
difficult a point I have written about before. The best time is in
bright weather in June, when the midday sun is high in the sky
and illuminates the rocky walls to best advantage.

The standard of climbing is certainly not high – only scram-
bling – with no great sense of exposure. Even so, it is well to
remember that a fall here could be serious, especially if one
were alone in poor visibility. The gritstone is here mainly thick-
bedded and coarse with much evidence of pebbles. Erosion by
water and by frost has produced the typical stairway in this
steeply-angled drainage channel. The level strata gives the flat
'treads' above each step, and the actual bedding is clear on the
vertical faces of these steps. Lining the plunge pools is the pale
gritstone powder worn from the upper clough and deposited
here by the stream.

My first encounter with this clough was on the return leg of
the Edale-Marsden Double some years ago. On that autumn
afternoon thick mist lay upon Bleaklow, and heavy rain had
turned the stream into a powerful torrent. Avoiding the largest
cascades slowed progress. But on a warm June day after a dry
spell there is but a lazy trickle here, and for much of its length
the water disappears altogether. This is the best sort of time to
explore at leisure this finest of all south Pennine cloughs.

At about fifteen hundred feet above sea level the steepest section ends and falls back at an easier angle towards the plateau-top of Bleaklow. It is at about this altitude that the heather
moor of the lower slopes, just above Longdendale, changes to
cotton-sedge moss resting on the less well drained peats right
up to the broad two-thousand-feet summit ridge. From this section of the clough you can look out north-westwards across
Longdendale to the sunlit dale drained by the Crowden Great
Brook, with the extensive gritstone exposure of Laddow Rocks
beyond. The broad plateau-top above Laddow Rocks is Black
Chew Head (1,774 feet), and Black Hill (1,908 feet) rises
beyond on the right. The Youth Hostel at Crowden is plainly

visible with the Pennine Way climbing diagonally right under the tree-dotted slope by Hey Edge towards Black Hill.

At least half of the total length of the stream draining this clough flows gently on the sloping northern shelf of Bleaklow. From about 1,750 feet the watercourse is edged with bilberry and cloudberry, bright and shiny in early summer. I recall a fine June day when we saw a vast murmuration of starlings come rushing in over the clough, a deafening aerial choir which moved at speed as one bird; then the flock was gone from sight. As we neared the two-thousand-feet contour, a family of friendly whinchats accompanied us, perching on rocks edged with the lush green of new bilberry growth. The same cloud of starlings came rushing over the moor again, their combined clamourings an unusual sound on these Pennine heights. Then, just as suddenly, they dropped to the plateau and were silent.

Next came a grouse family. The surprised chicks clustered by a boulder, cheeping excitedly while the anxious parents tumbled across the peat with their characteristic 'injury' distractions.

Where the highest channels in the peat indicate the source of the Wildboar Clough stream at nineteen hundred feet the call of the curlew signals that it is summer, that the waders have come up from shoreline and estuary to nest on the cotton-sedge mosses of highest Peakland.

14

Ewden and Bradfield

The Don is South Yorkshire's largest and most important river. Rising eight miles west of Penistone, it flows along the eastern edge of the Pennine country for some fifteen miles before entering the dark, industrial landscape of Sheffield. In this youthful stage the Don is joined by several eastward-flowing tributaries – the Porter or Little Don, the Ewden, Loxley and Rivelin among them. The most attractive of these east-west dales are those of the Ewden and the Loxley.

Ancient oak woodlands that once covered most of these steep valleys to the west and north of Sheffield were removed during the Middle Ages as a source of charcoal for the local iron-smelting industry. Today but small areas of these natural deciduous woodlands remain, one such being in the middle reaches of the Ewden Valley.

The Ewden Beck joins the Don where it meanders below Wharncliffe Wood between Stocksbridge and Oughtibridge. The stream has fallen about fourteen hundred feet in the seven miles from its source on the high watershed of the Pennines to the west. On the high ground overlooking the lowest part of the dale are two interesting settlements, one a village, the other a hamlet. The village is Bolsterstone, standing at almost a thousand feet on a ridge on the northern side, an ancient site with the remains of a Norman castle and a squat-towered parish church looking out across the dale to the Pennine moors. The hamlet is Brightholmlee, which occupies a commanding position above the southern mouth of the Ewden Valley; it is a collection of old cottages and farms with an attractive set of gritstone troughs beside the steep lane where horses and cattle are still watered.

Two reservoirs were constructed in this lower part of the

valley. The lower, More Hall, has a surface area of sixty-five acres and is used as compensation water for the Ewden Beck. Yachting enthusiasts find it very useful, and on a bright day the colourful sails make a grand sight below the frowning, gritstone moors. The upper water is Broomhead Reservoir, which has a surface area of 123 acres. Its 1,100 million gallon capacity makes it the third largest of Sheffield's water-supply reservoirs. Both Ewden reservoirs were completed in 1929. As Broomhead Reservoir filled, an old farmer is reported to have observed that "It'll nivver owd watter, lad," and, sure enough, it was not until 1933 that serious leaks in the bed of the dam were finally sealed. The problem was caused by underground fissures and persistent slipping of the hillsides.

The little village of Ewden occupies the sunny, northern slope between the two reservoirs and is largely a grouping of water-board dwellings. The coming of the reservoirs caused particular changes to some of the old buildings on the southern slopes of the valley. The ancient farm of Dwarriden ('the dwarf's dean' or 'hollow') was the home of the Ronksleys from about 1685 to 1935, when it became empty and was later demolished by Sheffield Corporation. The ancient cruck barn has been retained as a storage shed and is unique due to the great height of the stylobats (the stone bases for support of the cruck beams).

This site at Dwarriden, just south of Broomhead Reservoir, was obviously an important one, for it stands where two old trackways cross. Nearer Brightholmlee are two farms with ancient cruck buildings still standing. By the beck in the valley below stood Broomhead Mill (recorded in the thirteenth century) and New Mill (thus described about 1275) and remains of lead and zinc sulphide workings, but all have now disappeared since the coming of the reservoirs.

The ground steepens westwards of Broomhead Reservoir, rising four hundred feet to the edge of the open moors. On this slope and almost surrounded by planted coniferous forest stands Wigtwizzle, formerly an important hamlet of old farms with an interesting history but now reduced to one dwelling. It is known that Thomas Hall died at Wigtwizzle Hall Farm in 1644, leaving goods valued at £132. This dwelling had rare swan-neck carvings over four windows and was probably Elizabethan. Sheffield Corporation misguidedly demolished the building in 1936. Up to 1905 there was a public house here, but afterwards it became a farmhouse. It is a tragedy that what was once a delightful hillside settlement crouching sheltered beneath the eaves of the Pennines should have been reduced to a single smallholding and a few ancient outbuildings because of 'legalized vandalism' by a former planning authority.

Wigtwizzle stands at the edge of Broomhead Park, a spacious sweep of green sward dotted with ancient trees and an unexpected spot to find such a dignified landscape, an oasis lying between the open moors to the west and the steeper dale country below to the east. The original Broomhead Hall was built in 1311 and replaced in 1640 by a larger house erected by Christopher Wilson, a captain in the Parliamentary army. This must have been a most attractive house, but all that remains today is a pair of gateposts to the west of the recent building. This third dwelling was built in 1831 by James Rimington in the gabled Tudor fashion that was then becoming so popular. Later it contained the imposing early Georgian staircase from the Duke of Leeds' demolished Kiveton Park, near Rotherham – thought by many authorities to be the finest oak staircase in Yorkshire.

The Rimington Wilsons lived at Broomhead Hall until 1939, when it became in turn a school, insurance offices and a base for army units. After the war the only occupants have been farm workers, and since 1960 it has lain empty and was fast becoming a complete ruin, though the adjoining Home Farm and land is still tenanted. During 1977 the Hall was finally demolished. In early summer the gardens to the west and south of the house exhibit a mass of colour as the azaleas and rhododendrons bloom in turn – an arresting contrast with the windy moors across the Langsett-Bradfield hill road.

This north-south road crosses the Ewden Beck by means of a steep, hairpin bend and a narrow bridge. This really marks the boundary between the upper and lower parts of the dale. To the west the moors rise steadily to 1,750 feet and more on the watershed of Derwent Dale. Immediately upstream of the bridge, however, the beck flows in a densely wooded cleft. Rhododendrons form a thicket difficult to negotiate as one walks up by the cascading waters towards the head of Ewden.

Across the narrow defile of the dale, on the south side, is an impressive three-quarter-mile-long prehistoric earthwork and a cluster of Bronze Age tumuli. Here, too, is a stone circle that is difficult to find among the tall heather and summer bracken. The broad wilderness bounding the southern side of the upper Ewden is Broomhead Moor, formerly one of the richest grouse moors in Britain. The lonely shooting-cabin overlooking the Side Head Beck remains in good condition and is still used by shooting parties.

The uppermost reaches of the Ewden Beck wind through the peaty wastes of Upper Commons, a place which echoes to the call of the curlew, dunlin and stonechat in summertime; a dark, bleak landscape in winter. The gentle eminence of Pike Low (1,567 feet) commands the northern frontier of the basin and is topped by another prehistoric burial mound. The water tumbles in places down attractive little falls where the millstone grit rock outcrops. The several rivulets that join to form the Ewden begin life on the peaty slopes close to the summit of Margery Hill (1,793 feet), the highest point in South Yorkshire. From this height one can look westwards into Derwent Dale and eastwards down the broad hollow of Ewden Dale towards the green lowlands of the River Don.

One must walk some distance southwards from Margery Hill, along the watershed between Derwent and Don, to the broad and rather featureless top of Featherbed Moss (1,789 feet) to be able to see eastwards and south-eastwards into the large, smooth hollow of Bradfield Dale.

The largest of the valleys west and north-west of Sheffield is this lovely Bradfield Dale, drained by the River Loxley. It is more than eight miles from the source of the Strines Dike on Derwent Edge (one of the major headwaters of the Loxley) to the confluence of the Loxley with the Rivelin at Malin Bridge, one of Sheffield's north-western districts. It is nine miles from the source of Hobson Moss Dike (under Featherbed Moss) down the Agden branch of Bradfield Dale to Malin Bridge – both arms are considered part of this valley.

Bradfield Dale is a large hollow, and a whole book could be written about its past and present, its structure and scenery and the activities of its natives through the centuries. The complexity of its steep and sinuous lanes is well known to Sheffield folk, a pattern which I associate with that of the Ashover district; and in many ways it is a similar dale, though Bradfield Dale is more truly Pennine in character than the trough of the Amber, its heights greater and its upper farms more bleakly set.

G. H. B. Ward – 'the King of Ramblers' – considered the views overlooking Bradfield Dale from the vicinity of Holdworth and Cliffe House Farm (a mile south-east of Bradfield parish church) "the choicest surprise view of dale and moor within six miles of any large industrial city"; and the view from the footpath crossing the slope from Cliffe House Farm towards Bradfield church he stated, in the 1939 edition of *Across the Derbyshire Moors*, to be unequalled anywhere in the Peak District. It is a vista of the broad valley, wooded slopes towards the west beneath the high moors and the four large reservoirs in the Bradfield complex – a nice view, but I cannot agree with G. H. B. W. that it is unsurpassed in this region, being rather drab and cold when the sun is not shining, and when it is, the observer is looking into the bright light; give me a north-facing slope from which to see the best vistas, with the sun behind me and the things I am observing strongly illuminated. Do not misunderstand me, though: there are grand views from this slope near Bradfield, but they are not pre-eminent in the southern Pennines.

There are really two Bradfield settlements, near the place where the Agden Valley branches north-westwards. Low Bradfield lies beside the flood plain of the Loxley. It is a collection of old houses and cottages, and a steep, high-walled lane climbs the valley side at a gradient of one in five to High Bradfield, which is the true heart of the old village. The first reference to Bradfield village was, apparently, in 1188, but there is evidence of earlier settlement in the earthwork of Castle Hill a short distance south-east of the village. This may have been a look-out or watchtower, but it has never been proved that a true fortification occupied the site.

A much more important remnant lies a few hundred yards to the north-west of the church. This is the mound of Bailey Hill. Some authorities have considered this mound and moat the remains of a Saxon moot hill for assemblies, but the general opinion and probable origin is that this was a defensive site subsequently used by the Normans for a garrison and defensive base. G. H. B. W. refers to Bailey Hill as "the best local example of a British or Celtic burial mound", and if this is a correct assumption, it seems likely that the powerful Norman Roger de Busli (of Tickhill) gained possession of it soon after the Conquest.

The ridge-mound of Bailey Hill measures 310 feet and reaches a maximum of forty-five feet above the base of the adjacent trench. The height from the trench mound to the top of the circular mound on which a wooden structure was presumably placed is eighty feet. About 1720 a man called Jeremy Fairest is said to have attempted some excavation here but instead of finding the hoped-for treasure succeeded in exposing only "earth and squared stones with marks of the tool on them". If Bailey Hill did serve as a Norman fortification from which the district could be controlled, it could not have been used for long, largely because other military positions (such as Peveril and Sheffield Castles) could do the job adequately. In 1893 the eminent archæologist General Pitt Rivers had the site scheduled as an ancient monument.

The adjacent parish church of St Nicholas stands in a fine position with wide views of Bradfield Dale and is one of the largest in Hallamshire. The tower is fourteenth century, with pinnacles, and the whole building is attractively embattled (somewhat like the smaller church at Baslow) which gives a defensive appearance completely in keeping with the situation so close to the windy hills. There was a church here at the beginning of the thirteenth century but all points to a complete rebuilding during the following century, the result of which we see largely today. Associated with the church is the Turie Library, about 225 books in Greek, Latin and English bequeathed by the Reverend R. Turie, vicar of Ecclesall, in 1720. The ravages of time and some carelessness seem to have caused a steady reduction in the collection so that by 1966 there were only thirty-three volumes left, published between 1600 and 1707. The remains of the Turie Library are kept at the Rectory.

From most places in High Bradfield there are good views down into the dale, views which include one or more of the four reservoirs which lie in the floor of this broad trench. Near the head of the valley is Strines Reservoir; below it is Dale Dike and, some distance below Low Bradfield, the lowest is Dam-flask, while Agden Reservoir fills the lower reaches of the tributary Agden Valley. The most famous of the Bradfield reservoirs is Dale Dike.

Until early in the fifteenth century the small population of Sheffield was supplied with water by springs at the Ponds and at Westbar. In 1434 Barker's Pool was formed at the place called Balm Green, then a wooded suburb of the town, and this satisfied the area for over two hundred years. About 1743 small dams were built in the lower reaches of Crookesmoor Valley, thereafter other dams were formed in the same area. In 1830 an Act of Parliament constituted a water company, and dams were constructed at Crookes and Redmires.

Turning their attention to the Bradfield Valley, the water company now began to build a reservoir some distance above Low Bradfield, impounding the upper reaches of the Loxley (here called the Dale Dike), and this was finished in the winter of 1863–4. The rapidly expanding population of Sheffield needed more water immediately, so the directors of the water company resolved to fill the new Dale Dike reservoir as soon as it was completed. This impounding wall was twelve hundred feet long and almost a hundred feet high in the centre; it held 700 million cubic feet of water, and the surface of the reservoir covered 78 acres. The engineers responsible for this impressive dam believed, from tests carried out during construction, that the impounding wall could withstand ten times the pressure required of it when full of water.

It is recorded that "a heavy rainfall filled the dam rapidly, and a high wind, blowing down the gorge, hurled the water against the embankment in heavy waves." That was on 11th March 1864. During that afternoon the resident engineer carefully inspected the dam and then went back to Sheffield, satisfied that all was well. But an hour after the engineer's inspection a workman crossed the impounding wall and saw a horizontal crack in the outer slope. He reported this to the contractor. As no water was leaking, the contractor considered this to be simply a frost crack; however, he opened the outlet pipes and sent his son on horseback for the engineer. A short distance down the valley the saddle-girth broke, and the young man stopped in Damflask to repair it; telling the people there of the crack in the reservoir wall, he set off again for Sheffield. The population of Damflask were keenly interested by the news (and probably not a little anxious), and some of them set off in the gathering darkness to see for themselves.

It was ten o'clock by the time the resident engineer arrived, and the crack had now widened to such an extent that he immediately attempted to breach the overflow weir with gunpowder. His first effort did not work, and before another could be made the centre of the dam broke, sending a deluge of water down towards Low Bradfield. It was midnight. Contemporary records state that the flood water "swept like an avalanche down the course of the River Loxley to Hillsborough, and down the Don through the town, deluging the valleys on both sides to the depth of many feet".

In the region of Low Bradfield the water must have been from twenty to thirty feet deep as it swept all before it. The news of the cracking dam wall had spread quickly in the Bradfield neighbourhood and in Damflask, too, so that with the thunder of the breaking dam everyone thereabouts fled up the slopes to safety – all that was, except an infant washed out of its mother's arms at Low Bradfield and a labourer at Damflask who had scoffed at ideas of danger, gone to bed as usual and drowned; he was found "buried in debris far down the valley next day".

Below Damflask hamlet, however, word of the dangerous state of the reservoir had not been spread, and it was in the lower reaches of the Loxley Valley that most loss of life occurred. A record of the catastrophe written about thirty-five years after the event (1899) tells of the sudden terror which struck men and boys on night shift in the works near Malin Bridge: "Upon them in the darkness the deluge came as a terrible surprise, sweeping away many of the works and overwhelming the workers in their bewildered attempts to escape." A farmer by the name of Trickett, with his wife, several children, servants, father-in-law and a lodger lived in a large stone house where the River Loxley joins the River Rivelin at Malin Bridge. A neighbour living higher up the slope saw the foaming flood approaching "like a mountain of snow". The water struck the Trickett house and shook it "like a cradle". Lights were seen to flicker in the windows, and shrieks were heard from the terrified occupants. Then the whole house sank under the flood and was totally destroyed. Everyone was killed. Fifteen cottages nearby were swept away, too, and only three of their seventy inhabitants survived. That record of 1899 continued to explain that such destruction occurred all the way down the Loxley Valley from Damflask hamlet to Malin Bridge and Hillsborough, and "scenes in the valley of the Don at Owlerton and Sheffield were scarcely less harrowing." At Neepsend an Irish labourer got his wife and six children up onto the roof of his low, white-washed cottage, but the flood rose quickly and lifted the roof off, carrying them all away to be drowned.

One of the reasons for the extensive damage as far down the Don Valley as Sheffield was that the torrent came suddenly, without any warning or explanation. Loaded with much large wreckage the water "thundered against doors and walls like a battering ram". Within half an hour the flood had passed, carrying many of the drowned miles downstream towards Doncaster. The scene it left behind was described as one of "death and wreck and desolation almost unparalleled in the annals of English towns".

Altogether 4,511 houses were flooded, thirty-nine of which were totally destroyed and 376 partly destroyed. There were 240 persons killed, making this a far greater disaster than the bursting of the Bilberry Reservoir near Holmfirth twelve years earlier when eighty-one people were drowned. Unlike these east-facing valleys draining towards the Don, the Holmfirth Valley has had several serious floods causing loss of life through the years, including the cloudburst of 1944 when five people were drowned.

After the Dale Dike disaster the mayor of Sheffield launched an appeal, and quite quickly more than £55,000 was subscribed, more than enough to meet all urgent claims. The water company was ultimately found to be fully responsible for the event and had to pay £276,918.11s.7¾d for loss of life, personal injury and damage to property and trade. In addition they had an enormous sum to find for legal expenses and to commence construction of a new dam. As a result of the parliamentary campaign which ensued, the water company was authorized to add twenty-five per cent to its water rates for twenty-five years and allowed to borrow £400,000.

The cause of the collapse of Dale Dike dam wall was never fully discovered, though a committee of "five eminent engineers" decided that there must have been "a landslip on the east side of the embankment, extending under a portion of the outer slope". Before the dam had collapsed, the water company was already engaged in building the Agden Reservoir immediately to the west of Bradfield, and this work now continued. In 1869 this, ultimately the second largest of the Bradfield reservoirs, was finished. Two years earlier (and three years after the disaster) the Damflask Reservoir was completed on the site of the destroyed hamlet of that name. This is the largest of these man-made lakes, with a surface area of 115 acres and containing 1,158 million gallons.

Work re-commenced on the Dale Dike dam, and a new wall was built four hundred yards upstream from the original site, reducing its capacity by one-third. This was finished in 1875. Four years previously the Strines Reservoir was completed near the very head of the dale and not far down the slope from the ancient Strines Inn.

High up on the southern slope of the dale, a mile above the confluence of the Loxley with the Rivelin, stands the tiny hamlet of Little Matlock, so named "from the similarity it bears to the beautiful town of Matlock". I am afraid I cannot see this – the Derbyshire Matlock is a valley-bottom settlement; it lies in limestone country; it is a fair-sized town. And, anyway, this small spot, though so close to Stannington and Loxley and other villages which can now only be called parts of Sheffield, is a far nicer place to be or to visit than that larger over-rated spa threaded by the A6 highway.

The original name for Little Matlock was Cliffe-Rocher, after the extensive rock outcrop which extends westwards from the hamlet for half a mile. This is partly a natural landslip but largely a worked-out quarry used during the last century for building-stone. It is now thickly wooded, and there are now only limited views through the trees, out across the River Loxley towards Loxley Common and up the dale to Bradfield.

To Little Matlock my maternal grandfather took his new bride to make their home in the last years of the nineteenth century, for the hamlet formed part of the family's estate. My grandparents Reuben and Mary Dearden lived in Cliffe Cottage, which still stands adjacent to the Robin Hood Inn. At that time my grandfather managed the quarry for his brother-in-law, Job Holland. There were born my Aunt Joan and Uncle James (Dob) before my grandparents came back to live in Dronfield, grandma's home, about 1904. My grandfather made an aquarium in one of the Cliffe Cottage windows, trapping water between the window pane and a sheet of glass flush with the inside wall. The sight of goldfish swimming in a cottage window was, it seems, a great attraction for visitors out walking at Little Matlock on Sunday afternoons.

The hamlet has been thought by many to be situated in the 'Locksley Chase' so well celebrated in Robin Hood balads; it has often been reputed to be the birthplace of Robin Hood himself, and several wells in the district have the name 'Robin Hood's Well' – the outlaw must have had a tremendous thirst!

My grandfather's eldest brother was Hardress Dearden, who inherited the Little Matlock estate, and he was a friend of the antiquarian Johann Zimmermann who lived in the Sheffield district in the last century (though of Swiss origin) and who wrote *Historical and Antiquarian Sketches of the Neighbourhood of Sheffield*. Volume One described "The Loxley and the Rivelin" and was published by Pawson and Brailsford in 1863. The copy in front of me as I write is inscribed "To my friend Mr Hardress Dearden, High House, a gift of the author", and I can only conclude that it was presented years after publication because my great-uncle Hardress was born later than 1863. It is stated that the large house at Little Matlock was built about 1800 by a man called Halliday, a stone house "devoid of architectural beauty". This has long been 'The Robin Hood' public house, and Johann Zimmermann mentions that

there hangs a rude, and now nearly obliterated, sign of the famous outlaw, who is supposed to have been born in the neighbourhood. You can still distinguish the outlines of two figures, clad in what were once bright green tunics, with hunting-horns suspended from their girdles. One of them seems to be in the very act of blowing a long fierce blast – doubtless to summon his trusty followers from the surrounding woods. These we suppose are faithful representations of Robin Hood and his stalwart companion, Little John, or, as he was more properly called, John of Loxley, or Locksley, of the old ballads – who, tradition says, lies buried in the churchyard of Hathersage, a village about ten miles distant.

Now Hardress Dearden was a keen rifleman and was one of the founders of the Sheffield Rifle Club at the beginning of this century. As the owner of the old quarry at Little Matlock, he was instrumental in having the rifle range constructed there between 1900 and 1906. Before that time the Club shot indoors at the old Corn Exchange in Sheffield and out of doors at Edale. Its first President was, incidentally, Colonel Sir Howard Vincent, MP for Central Sheffield.

When the new rifle range was opened in 1906, the Robin Hood Inn was used as the Club's headquarters. Summer meetings were held under canvas at Filey. After the Second World War the 4th Derbyshire Home Guard Rifle Club used the Little Matlock Rifle Range for competitions, and it is from that period that I have clear memories; of warm Saturday afternoons when I went with my father, the late Lt. Col. Arthur L. Redfern, to the quarry clothed with trees; of far views across the dale to the white symmetry of the cemetery at Loxley; of walking with my father and the laughing Jimmy Johnstone who had a trim, grey beard and a jaunty tweed hat laden with shooting trophies and badges. He was a retired boiler-inspector who had come originally from Scotland but had lived at Loxley for a long, long time and travelled the world looking at steam-boilers. Jimmy Johnstone looked for all the world like General Smutts, and for me his laughing countenance on the rifle range at Little Matlock will never fade.

Another memory is of Matt Furness and his wife chatting to us in the cool shade of 'The Robin Hood'. The Furness family had been landlords of the inn for a long period, and Matthew was closely associated with the Sheffield Rifle Club. After Little Matlock was sold by my mother's family after the Second World War the Robin Hood Inn was purchased by Stones Brewery, which later merged with the Bass-Charrington group. The old inn was rapidly going derelict in the early seventies but, happily, a preservation order was placed on it, and the brewery has restored it. While work was going on there the former rifle-room upstairs was cleared out.

It had seats around the perimeter of the room with lockers under them, where the club members could safely leave their personal things while shooting on the range. In the middle of this upper room one of those almost-forgotten, portable air-raid shelters was standing, and to the corners of this were attached vices to hold rifle barrels while they were rodded and cleaned. Perhaps the most interesting find was made in the loft beneath the roof – five old photographs of Sheffield Rifle Club members. Three of these were apparently beyond repair, but two were sent to a picture-restorer and, I believe, are now hung in a public room of the Robin Hood Inn – perhaps the most appropriate place for them, though I suppose that few now looking at them ever knew them or know their life story which fades in detail and relevance with each passing year.

I recently went back to Little Matlock on a sort of sentimental journey. It was a cold, grey early spring day; there was not much colour in the landscape, and less in the heavy sky. The whole range was covered by a thicket of surprisingly large trees, and when I found the butts I recognized the rusting metal frames that once held the targets, and the underground shelter for those working them. But the trees were so thick that I wondered just how long it was since the range had been used.

The range had never had a safety certificate, and when new regulations were brought in it was found that the club would have to find between one and two thousand pounds to place safety netting around the area. The rent had been increased, too, and finally in 1958 the Sheffield Rifle Club left Little Matlock and have subsequently used the Territorial Army Rifle Range at Totley. Walking back through the trees to the two-hundred-yards firing-point, I thought I heard the laughing voice of Jimmy Johnstone, but it was a distant magpie. It was, of course, wishful thinking, for Jimmie was an old man when last I saw him, and the secretary of the rifle club later told me he had died in 1952. Uncle Hardress, Matt Furness, Jimmy Johnstone, my father – never again will they be seen on this woody hillslope; only their shadows cross between the trees, and, alone, I walked on quickly to Little Matlock and found there Cliffe Cottage with its windows bricked up and serving as a stable. It was a relief to climb the field above the Robin Hood Inn and find Bill Earnshaw at home at Stannington, a retired quarryman who knew so well those faces from the past.

Up near the head of Bradfield Dale, high overlooking the Strines Reservoir, is the remotely situated Strines Inn, at one thousand feet above sea level. This building is of great age and is known to have been the home of the Worrall family early in the sixteenth century. The arms of this family are carved in stone over the doorway, a lion rampant between three cups, impaling on a chevron three trefoils; in chief an arm in armour, embowed between two wings, holding a dagger bendwise within a bordure engrailed; crest on a helmet with mantling, a cup.

The inn dates from three building periods – the earliest now visible is probably sixteenth century; the next is the upper wing and is late-seventeenth century; and the most recent is the smallest part erected in 1860. Johann Zimmermann found the modern addition in bad taste, "built purely on the utilitarian principle, without any regard to its keeping with the other parts of the edifice" and found it impossible to forgive the landlord for building this room. Over a century later we can, I think, accept this part as fairly antique.

A few yards north of the Inn, at the top of the steep hill down to the Strines Brook, is an old roadside stone with "Take Off" inscribed on it. Johann Zimmermann considered this a marker to tell travellers where to strike off across the moors, but this is completely wrong. It was the place where the extra 'chain' horses were taken off after helping to haul a load up the gradient.

Strines has its tragedies and its humorous stories. Over two hundred years ago a travelling tailor came up here on his rounds after doing work in Bradfield. He had been seen there with some gold ornaments and, on reaching Strines, decided to spend the night at the inn because darkness had overtaken him. He was never seen again; rumours surrounded this disappearance, and many believed the landlord to know more than he admitted, but the mystery was never solved. On another occasion, when the Worralls lived at Strines, a practical joke went wrong. Apparently two young women dressed up as men and set out to impersonate the lover of one of the inn's maids. One of the girls was too nervous to go up to the house and hung back in the shadows, but her more confident friend went round to the back of the inn and whistled to attract the maid servant. The Worralls heard the whistling, and a window opened and a shot-gun was fired at what was thought to be a burglar. An old book records that "the figure was seen to reel and the shrieks of a young girl were heard." Only then did the landlord realize the mistake. The dead girl's ghost is said to be seen periodically at the back of Strines Inn.

Another story relates to a Bradfield tailor called Godfrey Jubb who is buried in Bradfield churchyard. During the eight-eenth century Godfrey went up to Strines to do some tailoring. In those days it was normal for such travelling tailors to stay for perhaps two or three days with the families for whom they were doing work, until the job was done. On this occasion Godfrey finished his work late in the evening and, remembering the disappearance of the travelling tailor already mentioned, began to have qualms about meeting his ghost which was said to haunt the premises and neighbourhood "and had often been seen on the bank-side below the house". Eventually Godfrey Jubb set off, but after he had gone some way he saw a figure clothed in white standing motionless in the middle of a field. He became terrified and raced back to Strines. The landlord "picked up a heavy bludgeon and determined to accompany Godfrey to the scene of his fright". As they approached the white figure in the moonlight, the frightened tailor fell behind the landlord who, coming close to the object, delivered a heavy blow with the bludgeon. The ghost materialized into a tall white thistle and its down flew in all directions. Poor Godfrey had had more than enough and readily returned to Strines with the landlord until next morning.

15

Winter on the Heights

The late Professor W. H. Pearsall has shown that soils will normally be waterlogged if rainfall regularly outpaces evaporation or, on steep gradients, run-off. He went further, suggesting that in the British context a rainfall of fifty to fifty-five inches (about 1,350 millimetres) the soil conditions will favour bog formation. If we consider the long-term rainfall records for Woodhead, at the head of Longdendale, we note an annual total of 50·2 inches (about 1,250 millimetres) and Woodhead is only about eight hundred feet above sea level. The highest parts of the gritstone plateaux around are a thousand to twelve hundred feet higher, so we can easily appreciate that the rainfall figures for those parts are likewise considerably more.

The driest months in Longdendale are April, May and February in that order, the wettest are October and November. The fairly level plateau country and the high rainfall allied to low rates of evaporation mean that large parts of the gritstone areas of the south Pennines consist of bog, commonly tussocks of cotton-sedge and often mixed with heather, sphagnum moss and bilberry. The common incidence of the name 'White Moss' (as, for instance, a mile west of Wessenden Head) suggests that the cotton-sedge has been established since ancient times – the common cotton-grass (*Eriophorum augustifolium*) paints white many of the acid moors of the southern Pennines in early summer when it blooms literally by the square mile.

Such dazzling acres under a sunny sky are a pleasure to walk over, but so often the summer skies of the gritstone heights are darkened by palls of cloud, and the widespread sheets of cotton-grass blooms are soggy on close acquaintance. The average annual sunshine total for the plateaux surfaces is less than a thousand hours.

Whereas the high plateaux of the south Pennines experience a precipitation of sixty inches (1,500 millimetres) and more each year compared with only thirty-four to forty inches (875–1,000 millimetres) on the lower limestone plateau to the south, it is perhaps surprising to realize that the highest precipitation is in the lee of the highest ground. One might expect the highest rainfall (and winter snowfall) to be on the steep, west-facing flanks of the hills, about Saddleworth or Glossop or in Cheshire's Wildboarclough. This is not so, for valleys like the Ashop and the Alport regularly record the highest annual precipitation, probably because of the phenomenon known as 'air mass convergence' which leads to instability of the moisture-laden atmosphere.

Taking this theme one stage further, it is pertinent to note that there is, on average, ten inches (250 millimetres) more precipitation in the vicinity of Edale Head at the western end of the Vale of Edale than in the lowest reaches of the same lowland only six miles to the east. In the same district the common winter phenomenon of temperature inversion causes interesting temperature differences between valley-floor and plateau-top. For instance, in the Ashop Valley in still, anticyclonic conditions, night temperatures of 18°F have been recorded at the same time as temperatures of as much as 40°F have been recorded on the plateau surface at Seal Edge, nine hundred feet above the Ashop. It is in such crisp weather that the heights are at their winter best, for, generally speaking, the gritstone country does seem to attract and retain masses of thick, grey cloud. On average the two-thousand-feet contour in the south Pennines has a seventy-day annual snow expectancy. Dr Alice Garnett has pointed out that the total time when the temperature falls below the growth threshold (42°F) is ninety per cent in January and February on this high ground. Some of this protracted period of low temperatures is due to a lack of radiation when the sun is obscured by those dense cloud masses, most of them condensing in from the west and southwest.

However, when the clouds disperse and the sky is revealed bright and clear above the dark winter hills of moor and edge, when snow lies brightly on the land, we are reminded of the blowing blankets of summer cotton-grass. It is often a matter of

luck if one manages to go up a gritstone valley in the right conditions and so reach the high ground on a day when the sky
remains clear and the atmosphere retains invigorating crisp-
ness. So often, as we well remember, the clouds gather and
darken the countenance of the land; we finish our day in thick
mist or beating rain or, at least, crossing a drab and darkened
moor with snow falling heavily on every side. When our winter
day remains perfect to the end, we have reason to be thankful
and to remember it well.

Here are just two memories of winter days on the gritstone
heights, when things went just as expected and when things
turned out adversely. The reader might consider what follows
to be something of a lesson to those traversing high ground in
winter conditions.

First, the day overlooking Cheshire's Wildboarclough when
things went well.

The road up to the Cat and Fiddle Inn from Buxton was very
icy, but the prospect down to the north, into the shaded confines of the Goyt Valley, was enticing, for the eastern sun was
catching the snow blankets on Hoo Moor. When we gained the
1,690-feet watershed at 'The Cat and Fiddle' the western hills
lay revealed in all their finery – as beautiful as ever I have seen
them. Wildboarclough was hidden, but the top of Macclesfield
Forest stood as a dark outline on the snowy ridge above White-
hills Farm and Forest Chapel. Beyond the white hills the grey-
blue haze of winter distance suggested the infinity of the Cheshire Plain. From the roadside here we set off on foot towards
the 1,834-feet summit of Shining Tor, now the highest point in
Cheshire. Grey and knotted boulders rolled away to left and
right as we walked on through the snow, sheep foraging for
molinia shoots beneath the crusty daub. In a mile we stood at
the top of Shining Tor and took in the lovely view again. How
still the world was on that morning, with few vehicles passing
below on the Buxton-Macclesfield road.

Cats Tor stands one and a half miles to the north, the next
high point on this gently undulating ridge. It is marked by quite
steep rocks on the western side. From the top of Shining Tor a
subsidiary ridge runs out towards the north-west, and between
these two arms there lies a deep hollow where the Todd Brook
rises. Down in this quiet, heathery basin are the ruins of lonely

Thursbitch Farm. When we came upon Thursbitch first many years ago, the golden light of a summer evening was flooding the basin, and a cuckoo was calling from Cats Tor. Looking down on that winter morning the area seemed full with new snow, sparkling stuff which reflected the frosty blue sky. Beyond Cats Tor we went down by Oldgate Nick and so crossed the ancient salt road out of Cheshire called The Street, and in a further mile we were perched upon Windgather Rocks.

The little Youth Hostel at Windgather is a grand spot, high on the hillside above the valley of the Todd Brook and Kettleshulme village. The vastness of the Cheshire Plain was hidden by a haziness which often accompanies frosty, anticyclonic conditions. Stockport and Manchester were quite obscured by that haze though the lovely features of near hill slopes, etched with curving snow and shadow, stood out sharply. It was a day to remember.

The sun cast long shadows from us as we went down into the valley, crossing the Todd Brook and on past Bummer Close to gain Blue Boar Farm at over thirteen hundred feet on its exposed hill-top. The narrow lane down to Nab End was thick with snow and, climbing a small drift, I was able to look over a high field wall and saw, not a dozen yards away, a flock of rooks tearing at the stiff carcase of a rabbit. Lamaload Reservoir was now in view to our right, still and rigid in its icy casing and dusted over with snow blown gently from the shoreline. As we walked on, eddies of powder snow twirled across the ice, and, beside the far shore, the black silhouette of a lone rambler appeared and disappeared through the stick-like outlines of empty trees. Beyond Lamaload the lane climbs steeply to the south and crosses the Buxton-Macclesfield road near Greenways.

Now the lane descends into Wildboarclough, and in no time we had reached Bottom-of-the-Oven where stand 'The Stanley Arms' (all this territory is owned by Lord Derby) and several renovated cottages. The sun which had shone all day was now dropping behind the Macclesfield Forest hills; a steel-blue shadow crept across our valley. We had expected a remarkable sunset but, as so often happens on clear days such as this, there was but a pale yellowing of the western sky, and then dusk gathered about us as we went southwards beside the Clough Brook.

Beyond Highash and the rhododendrons we came to Clough House Farm and there turned up the side-valley towards Cumberland Cottage. Beside the coniferous plantation in the last of the light with a star over the high moor ahead. Cumberland Cottage stands above the track, its only companions a group of gaunt trees which frame it nicely and make a good foreground with the conical height of Shutlingsloe (1,659 feet) a mile across Wildboarclough to the west. The spot was made to be photographed, but now a frosty zephyr rustled the needles on the conifers darkening our path on the right side. We went on up to the silent moor beneath that lone star. Turning to the north where two streams join, we came again to 'The Cat and Fiddle' as the last light left the sky far beyond Macclesfield. No cloud was visible, and the deep frost gripped our gritstone land; the day had ended as we had planned it – the snow had made us lift our legs, and our cheeks were pink and glowing.

The other winter's day I have in mind came in the middle of a long, snowy spell one January. Our intention was to walk the sixteen upland miles from Black Hill (at 1,908 feet then the highest point in Cheshire) south-eastwards to Derwent Edge and Ladybower. This is not a particularly arduous undertaking on a fine, dry day, but deep snow and drifts covered the land, and the weather forecast was not very optimistic. We were dropped on the 1,718-feet watershed at Upper Heyden on the Woodhead-Holmfirth road at 7 am and made our way in the darkness by the television station on Holme Moss and floundered on through deep drifts for over a mile to gain the triangulation station atop Black Hill. There was a cold wind blowing out of the south-west and thick mist swirled by fitfully. Turning back the way we had come, we made good progress back to the road for we had our footprints to follow.

The snow was deeper than we had expected, and we agreed that snow-shoes would have been ideal for our journey. We decided to modify our route to Ladybower, going straight down the Woodhead road and then up one of the steep cloughs draining the northern side of Bleaklow, cross the high watershed and find the upper reaches of the Westend Valley. It should then be relatively easy to go down that valley and so beside Howden, Derwent and Ladybower Reservoirs to Ladybower. Such a plan seemed preferable, avoiding much of the exposed ground where we knew the snow would be very deep. The revised route was a mistake and led us ultimately into trouble.

Daylight came in vaguely, a grey dawning through the thickest of cloud layers, as we went down the road to Heyden Bridge. In a further mile we came to Woodhead and turned eastwards in the direction of Sheffield. There was no traffic on this major road as we moved along it, making good progress for the next mile. Bleaklow's northern side was plastered with snow and looked more like a Highland mountain than a Pennine plateau. The road climbs up and over the western portal of Woodhead Tunnel, and where it curves around Ironbower Moss we went down steeply, crossed the River Etherow where the snow covered the ice and aimed for Middle Black Clough. Our aim was to follow this narrow valley to its head at Bleaklow Stones and thence go south-eastwards into the large hollow drained by the River Westend.

Low cloud came scudding over the moors from the southwest; a remarkably cold wind was blowing, and now and then flecks of snow fell across our faces. For some reason which I have never really discovered we ploughed on through the deep snow beside the silent stream and never turned leftwards up Middle Black Clough. Without realizing it, we walked on south-westwards towards the source of Near Black Clough. Had we taken the trouble to look at the compass, our mistake would have been quickly discovered. Once in a clough like this, though, it is easy to continue onwards, convinced that it is the correct valley and that no check on the route is necessary. As it was we went on, further from our intended route at each stride.

The snow got deeper as we climbed, and at two thousand feet the drifts were waist-deep in places. The odd flecks of snow which had fallen above Woodhead now became a steady fall of fine, powdery stuff, and visibility was quickly reduced to a few yards. On the summit ridge of Bleaklow the full force of the south-westerly beat upon our faces. The snow fell ever more thickly, and soon there was a blizzard raging at us.

We had, of course, left the confines of the clough and now must decide on a compass bearing to get us down into the headwaters of the Westend Valley – which we presumed to be only a few hundred yards to the south. In fact, these headwaters were a mile away to the east but we were not to know that. A compass bearing was taken, aiming, I recall, a few degrees east of south. We expected to go down through the white-out conditions and find some evidence of the streams which form the infant West-end. It was a great relief to feel the ground falling away ahead of us, and for a few moments there was a lull in the strength of the wind; the snow, too, eased, and we could make out the general form of a white hollow, albeit only vaguely. There was no time to lose in these improved conditions, though we were wet, cold and tired. We agreed to plough on until the valley below us offered some shelter from the blast and then to rest for ten minutes and eat some food.

A couple of minutes after the drop in wind-speed, we heard the next onslaught come roaring over the moor, and once again the blizzard broke around us with all its former fury. We were now down in that lonely hollow called The Swamp where several streams drain off the Bleaklow watershed to form the River Alport – this is the next major valley to the west of the West-end but we did not realize it. With the return of the gale the temperature dropped; even though we struggled on through the deepening snow blanket, we were cold, and the pelting snow sought out every crack in our armour. We were getting wet, and a difficult manœuvre with gloves and cuffs gave me a shock – it was 3 pm by my watch, and the failing light was caused not by thicker clouds but by the onset of dusk!

Now, had we been in the Westend Valley, a further two miles would have seen us on the hard road beside the large re-entrant on the western shore of Howden Reservoir; by 4pm, we judged, we should be on easier ground and the trouble-free walk down Derwent Dale. As it was, we had at least four miles to go, down through the narrow confines of Alport Dale where there is steep ground most of the way; once at Alport Bridge there would be more than five miles to walk along the A57 road to Ladybower.

Anyway, we had not discovered our route-finding error and plunged on through the wet stuff, heads bent against the snow-laden gale. As we went downhill we checked and re-checked the compass and discovered that our valley was curving towards the east and the wind was now blowing over our right shoulder; that, at least, was an asset to compensate for the quickly failing light.

We came to some large boulders and took shelter. This was the spot for our long awaited ten-minute halt. Food and drink made us feel stronger, despite soaked feet and frozen hands.

"I'll take my torch out of the rucksack in readiness," I said, placing it in an anorak pocket. It would obviously be needed soon, though the deep snow covering helped to keep our surroundings quite bright for some time to come. Then we were off again, making better progress even though the snow was up to our knees in places.

The ground fell away to our right, and it was possible to make out some distance below the dark shapes of rocks. We went down that way and found it to be a small cliff over which the river was still falling, its edges frozen into icicles and very beautiful. It was at that point that I had my first suspicions as to our whereabouts; this place was somehow familiar and was not a feature of the Westend Valley. It looked like one of the waterfalls high up in Alport Dale but I did not say anything. We quickly moved on, keeping the line of the river to our right. The wind was less strong down here, but the snow was still falling thickly.

Plugging on through the new snow was very tiring, and my eyes were tired after going all day through near-white-out conditions; now and then I saw brilliant flashes, a sure sign of strain after hours of exposure to feature-less snowscapes. Would we ever get down to a road that night? Would it be a long, cold night sheltering under a curving drift? We began to wonder now.

Turning a corner in our valley I saw a solitary tree just below me, and close beside it a small waterfall. This was definitely Alport Dale! Sweeping the far slope with the torch I hoped to pick out the broken ground of Grindlesgrain Tor, but the blanket of falling snow cut off the beam. We went on as best we could, sliding and slipping on the steep ground. It seemed several hours before the valley widened and the broadening floor allowed us to walk in comparative ease. At 7 pm we climbed up the track to Alport hamlet and went on with lighter spirits to Alport Bridge.

It was snowing heavily again as we set off down the A57 road towards Ladybower. We expected to take a good two hours to reach our destination, but the road had been kept quite clear and we strode on down by Rowlee cross-roads and below Hagg Farm. A snowplough clattered by towards Glossop and we got into its tracks; easier walking.

The cold wind at our backs was a positive bonus now, and the snow slowly eased. By the time we crossed Ashopton Viaduct over the Derwent Dale arm of Ladybower Reservoir, the snow had stopped altogether and we were able to pick out one or two stars through small holes in the dark clouds. We reached Ladybower a little before 9 pm and got into the car we had left there early that day, before our journey on to Holme Moss. We had been hard at work for fourteen hours, and we had another hour's drive home on difficult, icy roads.

In retrospect it is easy to say that we should have carefully checked the confluence where Middle Black Clough joins Near Black Clough, but the weather was bad and familiarity does breed carelessness. I would not have believed it possible that anyone could miss such an obvious junction of streams on a clear day – but our day was not clear. Extra minutes there to check the map would have saved us literally hours later on, and much hard work. Then again, had we not changed our plans at Holme Moss, had we gone by Withens Edge and Salter's Brook Bridge to the upper reaches of the Derwent, we would have got into sight of the uppermost Derwent before the blizzard began. It would have been a simple matter then to have dropped into the dale and gone all the way down in comparative comfort to Ashopton Viaduct and Ladybower. All that is with the benefit of hindsight. One lesson that should be learned from that day's exploits is to check the map constantly when conditions are difficult. To economize on map-reading because it is too wet, too cold or too windy is to court problems later in the day.

16

Northern Moors

The extensive moorlands, cut by many little valleys, which sweep as the major watershed for thirty miles between Holmfirth and Skipton, between the northern limits of the Peak District National Park and the southern edge of the Yorkshire Dales National Park, have never been really well known by ramblers in general. In 1974 the South Pennine Park was designated and covers much of this very region. The main aim was to draw increasing numbers here and hopefully to relieve pressure from visitors on the National Parks to north and south.

Of course, this elevated millstone grit country has always been popular with a core of knowledgeable local ramblers and a handful of informed bogtrotters from further afield. With the creation of the Pennine Way, too, a steady convoy of long-distance walkers began to traverse these hills, albeit on a single, roughly north-south route.

The River Calder is the major river draining eastwards from the central part of this region, and its deep and sinuous dale has been used as a trans-Pennine routeway through the centuries. It is a densely-peopled trough, spoiled in the last two centuries by industrial development and associated trade-ways – road (A646), railway (Lancashire-Yorkshire) and canal (the now defunct Rochdale Canal). Hebden Bridge is the logical central settlement of the district, particularly so for the walker intending to explore the hills around. The topography is the making of the stone town, for the steep sides of the River Calder have forced ingenuity upon builders through the years – abrupt terraces, sudden inclines and buildings with basements and tall façades out over the valley. The tower of St James's parish church rises above the tributary called Colden Water, at the bottom of the sharp hillside, wooded, which rises

The late L. S. Lowry's studio (left) at the rear of 'The Elms', Stalybridge Road, Mottram-in-Longdendale (Chapter 17).

Looking north from the summit of Hollingworthhall Moor (1,309 feet) on an autumn afternoon (Chapter 17).

St Chad's church, Saddleworth, in the winter of 1947 (Chapter 17).

Fire at Bankfield Mill, Dobcross, Saddleworth, in January 1947
(Chapter 17).

The south portal of Standedge Tunnel, Huddersfield Narrow Canal, at Diggle (Chapter 18).

Bosley Locks on the Macclesfield Canal. (Chapter 18)

Hooleyhey Farm beside Lamaload Reservoir, upper Dean Valley (Chapter 19).

Adlington Hall beside the River Dean. (Chapter 19)

Kerridge Hill and White Nancy from Ginclough, above Rainow
(Chapter 19).

Red deer in Lyme Park (Chapter 19).

St Christopher's parish church, Pott Shrigley (Chapter 19).

The chimney of Dane-bower Colliery in the upper Dane Valley (Chapter 20).

The former Eagle and Child Inn at Burntcliff Top, looking towards Allgreave above the Dane Valley (Chapter 20).

The remains of Gradbach silk mill (Chapter 20).

The former Keeper's Cottage beside the Barlow Brook at Lee Bridge
(Chapter 21).

The path to the Bull Field,
Monk Wood, 1925 (Chapter 21).

Mary and Reuben Dearden, the
author's maternal grandparents,
at the Pig Gate, Monk Wood,
1920 (Chapter 21).

to the handsome upland village of Heptonstall. This latter is a breezy sort of place, on a narrow spur above the congested valleys, and only recently has it come to be generally appreciated as something of an architectural gem. The old church was dismantled in 1854 but, luckily, left to stand as a feature; the blunt tower has stonework from the thirteenth century and has been likened to a 'North Country tower house'. Its successor proved a large and costly affair, erected 1850–4, but it does not match the village half as well as the original church. There are many other interesting buildings, such as the sixteenth-century White Hall with three gables and good mullioned windows.

Ramblers using the Pennine Way often make the one-and-a-half-mile detour somewhere near Colden hamlet to take a look at Heptonstall and to buy provisions at Hebden Bridge. On a sunny day the detour is well worth the effort involved. For the walker seeking a pleasant day in this part of the Pennines, there are plenty of footpaths hereabouts, and some of them unusual in that they are paved with local stone and bounded with dry stone walls for the easier progress of pedestrians long ago, and to keep folk on the straight and narrow. There is, though, much evidence of stone wall and paved path neglect. Views down into the valleys are good, revealing steep woodland, tilted pasture and the brown-headed moors promising better things the higher one goes.

The majority of walkers seen in this district will, of course, be those engaged on the Pennine Way (in part or in whole). If they are going northwards, the descent into the Calder Valley will be the first section of low ground traversed since crossing Longdendale. From here northwards the terrain is less elevated and offers gentler progress, so Hebden Bridge and its valley can be thought of as the boundary between the really high ground which extends all the way to Edale and the valleys and lesser moorlands which stretch northwards before melting into the well-known limestone country beyond Skipton and the Aire Valley.

I am not going to describe in detail here the best walking routes on these northern moors, nor am I going to make more than a passing reference to the Haworth moors and Brontëland – there is not space, and more than enough has already been written about that subject. The point of this chapter is to mention a few of the really attractive places to which a rambler can make his own route.

The Pennine Way comes north from Standege to cross the M62 motorway on a high sweep of concrete and then passes the Post Office telegraph station on Windy Hill before curving off through appropriately named Slippery Moss to Blackstone Edge. Here is a fine exposure of dark gritstone looking out over Lancashire, the triangulation station being at 1,553 feet above sea level. Half a mile to the north again – half way to the Little-borough-Halifax road (A58) – an old route comes over the watershed, paved in parts and looking ancient. For a long time this was thought to be of Roman origin, but current opinion seems to think it is more likely to be a medieval trackway, rather as the so-called Roman Steps in the Harlech Dome, Gwynedd are now thought to be part of a medieval trackway. Anyhow, here on Blackstone Edge the Pennine Way crosses the old trackway at the famous Aiggin Stone, a guide-stone right on the watershed which now lies fallen on its side. For the walker aiming towards the north, the Aiggin Stone marks the start of what A. Wainwright correctly describes as "the easiest part of the Way". For three miles the path follows first the Broad Head Drain (as far as the famous White House Inn on the summit of the Littleborough-Halifax (A58) road) and then the Regulating Drain which carry water along at about 1,250 feet above sea level between Oldham Corporation's network of ridge-top reservoirs. One can walk along at a good speed here, and even in thick mist one can proceed with confidence beside these waterways.

The Pennine Way passes within a couple of miles of Turvin Clough, a little valley falling north-eastwards towards Mytholmroyd where the notorious Yorkshire Coiners lived and 'doctored' coins of the realm until their leader was hanged at York. At a sudden bend in the Warland Drain the easy going gives way to typically rough tracks, marked periodically with cairns which are jolly useful in poor visibility. The route goes down to a gentle col called Withens Gate where a paved way (similar to many on the flanks of the Calder Valley ahead) comes over from Withens Clough and its reservoir to Todmorden. Incidentally, half a mile down towards Todmorden stands Mankinholes, an upland hamlet where the Quakers gathered

as early as 1667 – one of the earliest records of their existence. It
is best known nowadays for its conveniently situated (busy)
Youth Hostel, one of the nearest to the Pennine Way there is.
The winding road which comes up the slope from Mankinholes
is often referred to as 'the Long Drag', a route planned by John
Fielden of Dobroyd Castle on the western slope of the valley adjacent to Todmorden. This philanthropic mill-owner had the
hill route made so that a carriage could be got to the summit of
Stoodley Pike, but the real purpose was to give work to mill-
workers who would otherwise have starved in the notorious
Cotton Famine; there are other examples of employers giving
similarly imaginative work to their men when times were hard.
Take, for instance, 'the Duke of Norfolk's Garden' above the
Shelf Brook, east of Glossop. Mill-workers were set to work to
dig a large piece of moorland with little hope of the ground
being much improved thereby, but the men did not starve and
retained their dignity – at least they had not been reduced to
paupers or even had to rely upon the parish.

Beyond Withens Gate the Pennine Way goes up gently, and
the route ahead is an open, airy one with the large monument
atop Stoodley Pike to entice you forward. This obelisk of dark
stone was erected on the site of an earlier landmark to com-
memorate Napoleon's abdication and the Peace of Ghent which
followed Waterloo. Work started in 1814, but about 1854 it fell
down. Reconstruction was completed to celebrate the end of
the Crimean War in 1856, but the tower makes an excellent
lightning-conductor and has suffered serious damage on several occasions, particularly in 1889. Having gained the foot of
the structure it is certainly worth the little extra effort to climb
the thirty-nine steps inside the base to reach the viewing plat-
form and look up the sides of the tapering needle. The whole
obelisk rises 120 feet above the top of Stoodley Pike and is an
obvious feature from miles around. There are many ways up to
it, including the short, steep climb up from the Calder Valley by
way of delightful Callis Wood and the clearest spring of water
(not far below the summit) on the Pennine Way since the Vale
of Edale. Another way up is from Mytholmroyd and the
wooded Cragg Valley, thence by Parrock Clough and onto
Erringden Moor.

To the north of Hebden Bridge the valleys of Hebden Water

and Crimsworth Dean are well wooded and in part owned by
the National Trust. They are understandably popular places,
and footpaths make access easy. Hardcastle Crags overlook the
Hebden Water, a busy spot on a fine Sunday afternoon, but the
Pennine Way proper keeps to the higher ground some distance
to the west of the valley, crossing the open flanks of Heptonstall
Moor to cross the valley below the Lower Gorple Reservoir.
The path ahead winds up the Walshaw Dean Valley, between
its three reservoirs before crossing open Withins Height (1,500
feet) and coming in sight of lonely Withins ('Top Withens' is
the old local name). This is the empty farm on the eastern slope
of the main Pennine watershed not far above Oakworth and
Haworth. In 1964 the Brontë Society placed a plaque on the
wall of Withins Farm which states:

> Top Withens
> This farmhouse has been associated with
> *Wuthering Heights*
> the Earnshaw Home in Emily Brontë's Novel.
> The buildings, even when complete, bore
> no resemblance to the house she described,
> but the situation may have been in her
> mind when she wrote of the moorland
> setting of the Heights.

This is the most outlying of popular Brontë associations, happily less visited than Haworth itself, but vandalism has in
recent times taken its toll of the bleakly situated house on the
moor. Of late much restoration has taken place here, and it is to
be hoped that the cared-for appearance will deter would-be
law-breakers and takers-away of Brontë relics (albeit ever so
tenuously linked.)

In a further mile the Pennine Way comes to Ponden, lonely
again above its narrow reservoir. The Hall stands in a fine position overlooking the reservoir and has most of the features
necessary to play adequately the part of Emily Brontë's
Thrushcross Grange. The house was built in two periods – the
earliest in 1634, the other in 1801 – and is lit with some fine mullioned windows. Sir Nikolaus Pevsner refers to the attractive
front gardens, made all the more romantic by high stone walls

punctuated with piers having finials of ogee outline. Inside there are good-sized rooms with sensibly proportioned fire-places and oak-beamed ceilings. As A. Wainwright points out, Ponden Hall is one of the very few dwellings actually on the Pennine Way which offers refreshments and overnight accom-modation. One does not need to have an over-developed im-agination to conjure up the atmosphere at Ponden Hall on a windy December night, when the bare trees near the farm are moaning in the fitful moonlight.

Northwards again, over Oakworth Moor and Ickornshaw Moor and down towards Cowling beside the Colne-Keighley road. This village (pronounced 'Cowlin' by the locals) has no great merit architecturally, its parish church of the Holy Trin-ity dating from 1845 with a bold, pinnacled tower. By the way, on the way down Ickornshaw Moor towards Cowling the two tall stone structures on nearby Earl Crag (a short distance east of the Pennine Way) will be obvious. They are the steep pyramid of Wainman's Pinnacle (nearest Cowling) and the solid-looking Lund's Tower with battlements overlooking the steep slope down to Glusburn and the Aire Valley.

There is space here to mention only one more fascinating corner of these moors which are virtually the northern boundary of our subject. This particular corner is pretty, and little-known, Lothersdale. The Lothersdale Beck and its little tributary the Surgill Beck drain a grand small-scale dale which opens out to the east. It is only about three miles long, and towards its upper end is the pretty, tree-shadowed and shel-tered village with its textile mill and cottages. The little church was built in 1838 and is no outstanding beauty, but half a mile up the lane towards Glusburn – one must climb to get out of this dale by road – stands the three-storeyed house called Stone Gappe, two centuries old and used by Charlotte Brontë as the model for Gateshead Hall in her *Jane Eyre*.

Looking to the west from all these moors in the Hebden Bridge district (and from the hilltops as far north as Lothers-dale), there are vistas to other uplands with a story of their own. These are the Forest of Pendle, dominated by the shapely pro-file of Pendle Hill (1,831 feet), the path-dissected Forest of Ros-sendale (south of Burnley and notable as the home of staunch Non-Conformists and hymn-writers long ago) and out towards

the Lancashire plain, moorlands with true Lancastrian names –
such as Darwen, Oswaldtwistle and Anglezarke. It is a pity that
we cannot explore them here, but that is another story.

17

Tameside

The confluence of the River Goyt with the River Tame marks the point where the Mersey comes into being. Some think the Goyt is the true headwater of the Mersey, while others argue that the Tame is the major parent-river. I favour the Goyt, so making the actual source of the Mersey on the open moor close to The Cat and Fiddle Inn, but I do not claim any particularly strong reason for this precedence over the Tame. The Goyt is no more important than the Tame.

The valley of the Tame is narrow and sinuous in its upper half, from the high moorland near Denshaw and Standedge down by Saddleworth, Greenfield and Mossley. At Stalybridge the hills fall back and the broad lowland extends all the way to Liverpool Bay, a lowland almost hidden by the Greater Manchester conurbation. The Tame flows on beyond Stalybridge, through Dukinfield, skirting Hyde to reach the Goyt at Stockport. The latter settlement, incidentally, developed at the spot where a Roman ford carried the Buxton (Aquae Arnametiae) road northwards. In Norman times there was a castle-site here, overlooking the beginnings of the Mersey, and about 1220 the Earl of Chester granted the lord of the manor, one Robert de Stockport, a borough charter.

It is, though, the upper reaches of the Tame valley which are Pennine in character. The steep-sided valleys are dotted with settlements and the scars of quite early industrial development. The Huddersfield Narrow Canal and the main railway route between Manchester and West Yorkshire pass this way, though the former has long been derelict.

Of course, until local government re-organization in 1974 there was a real anomaly in this district, for though the valley was geographically Lancastrian, and most inhabitants looked westwards to Manchester, the upper half of it, beyond Mossley, lay in Yorkshire's West Riding. A narrow tongue of Lancashire crossed the valley near Mossley, and to south of that was north-eastern Cheshire – an altogether unsatisfactory borderland arrangement considering the terrain of this district. Since 1974 the entire valley has lain sensibly within Greater Manchester, though many established inhabitants greatly resented leaving their beloved West Riding!

Up on the open tops above the Tame Valley one can see a long way in clear conditions; out over the plain of south Lancashire in one direction and across into the gritstone heights of the south Pennines proper in the other direction. These open little hills contain several interesting antiquities which make useful objectives when planning a walking route. At nine hundred feet above sea level a mile north-west of Diggle and overlooking the little moorland valley which goes down from the Pennine Way on Standedge towards Delph lie the remains of Castle Shaw Roman fort. It is a modest earthwork, all that exists to mark the presence of Roman forces in this head-valley and probably associated with the protection of a Roman route running northwards from Melandra Castle on the east bank of the River Etherow, near Glossop, but more definitely with the route from Manchester (Mamucium) to York. The fort is of two building periods, an outer turf and clay rampart enclosing $2\frac{1}{2}$ acres and dating from about AD 80 when the Roman general Agricola was Governor of Britain; the smaller, inner fortress measures only sixty yards by fifty yards and is slightly younger. It is thought to have been abandoned in the reign of Hadrian, say AD 125, for by this time the native warriors had been subdued hereabouts and Roman forces were required in the areas nearer Scotland which were still giving trouble. In any event, Castle Shaw would have been an unattractive place to be garrisoned for long. It is still so often a wet and cloudy district.

Five miles to the south and overlooking the eastern slopes of the Tame Valley are the remains of Buckton Castle. The site is 1,123 feet above sea level and immediately to the south-east of Mossley. This is not a castle ruin in the generally accepted sense but an earthwork of uncertain age. When walking over from the Tintwistle (south-east) district of Swineshaw Reservoir, there is a good view of Buckton Castle from the side of

Slatepit Moor. One is looking across the deep tributary valley of the Carr Brook, with its large works filling its floor. High up above this the steep hillside can be seen to be partially excavated. Actually much recent excavation has taken place on the eastern side of Buckton Castle, and this has rather spoilt the hill-top site and the view of it from this path on Slatepit Moor.

An old tradition had it that there was buried treasure within this castle, now only a weathered earthwork. In 1730 over one hundred people are reported to have gathered at Buckton Castle, and there they began "vigorous digging" over several days. No treasure was found, but as recently as 1908 traces of this digging were still visible. However, twenty or so years after the great dig various ornaments and a chain of gold beads were found quite accidentally beside the old road (now the B6175) down the slope to the west of Buckton Castle. About 1800 more gold beads were found quite close to the earthwork.

A mile north of Buckton Castle a large tributary comes down from the east, draining Saddleworth Moor and the western flanks of Wessenden Head Moor. It is called the Greenfield Brook, winding down through Greenfield to join the Tame one mile south of Saddleworth. This tributary valley is very steep-sided, its mouth guarded by conspicuous, gritstone headlands – Alphin Pike (1,544 feet) to the south and outcropped-topped Dick Hill where an obelisk stands sentinel by the rugged tors known locally as 'Pots and Pans'.

This sinuous, often dark, valley is best known for the huge Dovestone Quarry which overlooks its middle section. Derelict for many years, this exposure has long been popular with Manchester and Sheffield climbers as it represents one of the biggest gritstone faces in the Peak District and the entire Pennines. Like Wharncliffe Crags, near Stocksbridge, it lies on the leeward side of an industrial area and was rather a sooty crag to climb on; a general reduction in atmospheric pollution has lessened this nuisance at Dovestone Quarry.

The Greenfield Brook's major tributary is the Chew Brook. This latter flows in from the south-east and drains a large area of plateau due east of Laddow Rocks where in summer white blankets of blooming cotton-grass contrast with the peaty groughs and the shining waters of Chew Reservoir (at over sixteen hundred feet above sea level one of the highest reservoirs in the southern Pennines).

On a bleak autumn day we walked over from Tintwistle by way of Swineshaw Reservoirs to the place where Buckton Castle comes into full view high above the Carr Brook; and there, far below, the winding dale of the Tame lay suddenly revealed. Mossley is the central settlement in this vista, backed by the stone-walled hills towards Oldham. From all the high points in this area a dark tower is conspicuous on the heights just west of Mossley. This is Hartshead Pike. It seems likely that this site served anciently as a beacon and that there has been a stone structure here for centuries – certainly long before 1751 when the structure is reported to have been rebuilt. Lightning was probably responsible for the serious damage reported in 1794, when "the tower became rent from top to bottom." The tower fell into ruin over subsequent years, but on 17th September 1863 the foundation stone of a new structure was laid sixty-seven yards from the ruins of the old one. Three thousand people gathered on the hill-top that day to see the Mayor of Ashton-under-Lyme lay the stone over a bottle containing "coins, newspapers, verses by a local poet (James Dawson, of Hartshead) and a parchment record of the event". This particular year seems to have been chosen so that the new tower could double as a memorial to the celebration of the marriage of the Prince of Wales.

On 22nd December 1927 a great gale seriously damaged Hartshead Pike. A public appeal was launched the following year, and restoration was completed by November 1928. I remember that biting gale that buffeted us on that autumn day when we came over from Tintwistle. It was almost impossible to make ourselves heard, and the broad view we had hoped for was daubed with so much grey cloud that we saw only hazy distances out over southern Lancashire and colourless hill shapes towards the Pennine watershed. All this deeply incised country of Tameside can have a hard and unattractive countenance, nowhere more so than here on this Pennine outlier at Hartshead.

Though high valleys of central Peakland (notably the Ashop and the Alport) receive consistently higher rainfall, these western slopes of the southern Pennines do have more precipitation than their counterparts east of the main watershed. In winter cloud and rain seem to be far more common here than, say, in the Sheffield district. There have been some memorable snow-falls in Tameside, and my old friend E. Hector Kyme, who lived in the Saddleworth district for several years, recalls one twenty-four-hour period in January 1947:

'Waltzing Matilda' could well have been the theme song for the coach load of parents and teachers who were too tense for such activity when, 'whoish' and a subdued scream accompanied by the aroma of hot coffee, indicated that a thermos flask had become the victim of another skid. The hard-packed snow on the Huddersfield to Oldham road proved a fearsome track there on its highest stretch of the notorious Standedge.

Uppermill Square was clear as folk gathered for the round trip to a camp school at Pateley Bridge, and soon all who filled the coach were warm with excitement by reason of the dreadful driving conditions. A thousand times rather I would have gone by train through Standedge Tunnel some hundreds of feet below that nightmarish track past the 'Floating Light' and 'Great Western' Inns.

Having waltzed through the 'cut' which reduces the height of the infamous pass and the coffee flask smashing, the driver wisely decided (even to the fact of adding many miles to the journey) to keep to well-used urban roads, thus avoiding dangerous, hilly and winding ways already like skating-rinks.

'Steamed up' windows thankfully hid from view much of the hideous, grimy snow and slush as we swished through the towns, and, as for myself, I regretted missing the snowy ermine of expansive moorlands and upland fields, crossed and lined with twisting walls and dotted hereabouts with stark barns and farmsteads had we travelled as planned. Not for us the ethereal egg-shell-blue sky, or the scintillation of shining white roof-tops or of leafless trees praying to their maker adorned with their apparel of black and white surplices; no, it was WINTER, with the morbidity of a huge, glum oil-painting long overdue for cleaning, the last vestige of the landscape hidden from the viewers.

We carefully reached our destination in the Dales under the capable and silent and acutely attentive driver on a cold day of all cold days, having confirmed that a good, hot meal would be ready at Harrogate before returning home.

These fulfilments done, we were soon at Pateley Bridge. Down the steep incline and over the bridge, round a few corners and into the grounds of the Camp School.

Having greeted pupils and teachers, I sauntered around in spite of the cold and still recall the brilliance of moss on the bole of a huge tree; the steep-sided valley provided excellent growing conditions but not on a day like this. Photographs were impossible as from the inverted, leaden bowl of the heavens sporadic snowy petals fluttered down, ominous signs of abundance to come.

Shaking heads and hoarse whispers were indicative that we had better be off to arrive home safely and forgo the meal. Yet on arrival at Harrogate we had the bodily fortification for the journey in two sittings, and as some of us spent the waiting time, the twinkling lights revealed a township worthy of Switzerland for the new covering of snow and the falling flakes adorned lawns and garlanded trees and buildings alike so that the Town Beautiful on any occasion seemed like a newly-created city of scintillating icefloes risen to greet the Ice King.

The second sitting over and several travellers fortified with the 'spirit', all gathered on the waiting coach with trepidation for the spate of flakes was now obliterating all tracks – in fact, traffic seemed to have been wisely put into hibernation.

We shuddered off as the tyres churned in the newly fallen mass, and at a favourable incline the driver slid into a gear he could maintain unafraid of approaching traffic – though there was none! The glaring headlights spat defiance into the face of the white hostility, and but for hedgerows and walls setting ghostly limits we could have been on a plain of unchartered snow. We were guided only by the most skilful driving I have ever known through a blinding blizzard to Marsden at the foot of the terrifying Pennine road over Standedge towards Oldham.

The driver had only two alternatives – either choose a low gear and risk skidding to a halt and have all of us separated from the outside world in deep drifts or walk from Marsden and have us guided through the long and grimy Standedge railway tunnel to Diggle and so to Uppermill. The driver grimly maintained his seat and spoke to no one while the engine continued to purr like a contented cat. Never did man and machine respond more purposefully, until wildeyed headlamps met us on the homeward side of Standedge. We were through – to a cheer, and we knew now that we could get home. Above the subdued whispering there came from the driver an improvised tune; he was whistling now, a contented man who had succeeded after contention with fierce odds and won by the combined elements of skill and courage. 1947 was the worst winter in the memory of any living person.

Now all folk had to reach their homes safely after the wild

journey, and there from the vicarage windows shone a guiding light which lead the contingent across the wild, blizzard-swept fields. Returning, I took to the lane, almost full of the deadly shroud of deep whiteness. I fought in the drifts to my waist and was tempted to rest, but resolution urged me on to the road, knowing it could be fatal to stop. Perhaps there would be someone to accompany me on my last two miles home; but there was not.

Instead a frightening, intermittent shower of sparks confronted me at Bank Field Mill. It looked serious, and I considered returning one mile to Uppermill Police Station when muffled shouts indicated the matter was in hand.

The swinging cables between the high buildings caused miniature lightning, while ghastly gables, like devils' teeth, stood ghoulish amid the hissing sparks.

Only a quarter of a mile to home, to say I was safely back, hours late; I suggested that the family look from the bedroom window should a fire begin at the mill. Two fields away from the warehouse were new houses, and but fifty yards distant were work people's cottages. Every house nearby had now doffed its cap of snow from the roof as the fierce heat of the mill fire grew. As many dragons breathed fire as there were windows in the big building; and as floors gave way with rumbling roars, the flames of Hades seemed to assail the very Heavens. A field away I decided was near enough for a photograph so, with a wall to shield me in case the wind veered, I, too, doffed my hat to shield my face from the glowing heat.

What a day it had been. Hurling snowstorm, deep frost and the wilting heat of this blazing mill at dead of night.

In its last few miles before the confluence with the Goyt at Stockport, say from Dukinfield, the Tame must have once flowed through attractive, rural lowland. First industrial development and then sprawling suburbia have engulfed much of this flood plain so that the stranger wandering near Bredbury or Hyde nowadays would get little impression of the former beauty. There are, though, one or two remnants which give the game away, but they must be searched out.

Take, for instance, Hyde Hall, near Denton. It is a few hundred yards north of the tightly meandering river between Haughton Green and Denton. It exhibits two distinct building styles – the earliest probably dating from the thirteenth century and typically half-timbered. The later addition, maybe early-seventeenth century, is in dressed stone and includes the porch over the main entrance on the west side. It was the original home of the Hydes of Denton.

Close beside the River Goyt near Bredbury stands Goyt Hall, another half-timbered hall which was erected by Randel Davenport about 1570 as a mansion for the Davenports of Henbury. Another old building lies back off Huddersfield Road, Stalybridge. This is Stayley Old Hall, an Elizabethan yeoman farmer's dwelling in dark stone with three storeys, beautifully proportioned. The manor of Stayley was once known as 'Staveley' and is linked with the arrival of the Saxons and the Danes in England. The earliest mention of the Manor of Stayley is 1318, and it was conveyed to Robert de Stayley by Robert de Hough. The house remained in the possession of the Stayleys until 1471 when, the male line having failed, the only child, Elizabeth, married Sir Thomas Ashton of Ashton-under-Lyme. It has changed ownership since that time.

Not geographically part of Tameside but sufficiently close to include here is that part of lower Longdendale centred on Hollingworth and Mottram-in-Longdendale. The outstanding architectural feature of the district is without question the parish church of St Michael, Mottram, popularly known as 'the Cathedral of East Cheshire' (though now in Tameside, Greater Manchester). Few churches stand more conspicuously and dramatically above the settlement they serve than St Michael's does above Mottram, on account of the conical hill-top. The little stone town lies mainly to the west and north-west of this elevation, and the view from the churchyard is of a multitude of roof-tops and dark hills and the stern grandeur of Longdendale away beyond Hollingworth. On this hill-top where the church now stands, a battle took place in the twelfth century between King Stephen and Matilda, daughter of King Henry I, who contested the former's claim to the throne. Civil war raged for several years, and this engagement at Mottram was just one of many which finally ceased with the Treaty of Wallingford, whereby Stephen was allowed to keep the throne on condition that Matilda's son should succeed him (as Henry II), which he did in 1154 to become the first of the Plantagenets.

It is not known who founded the original thirteenth-century church here; most of the St Michael's we see now dates from the fifteenth century. Apart from the tall, dark tower, the best features are the two chapels within the building. On the north side is the Hollingworth Chapel, formerly the property of the old family of Hollingworth (or Hollyngworth) which took its name from the next settlement up Longdendale. On the south side is the finer Staley Chapel – finer, that is, because it contains two important sepulchral effigies in sandstone representing Sir Ralph Staveley ('Staley' and 'Staly' are more recent spellings of the name, hence Staveleys were lords of the manor of Staveley – now Stalybridge) and his wife, who were living at the beginning of the fifteenth century.

The exposed churchyard (it lies at 772 feet above sea level and catches every wind that blows) contains many interesting, often amusing, epitaphs. Take, for example, the one near the north-east corner of the church which refers to body-snatching –

> To wretches who pursue this barbarous trade
> Your carcases in turn may be convey'd
> Like his, to some unfeeling surgeon's room
> Nor can they justly meet a better doom.

One fruitful parishioner is recorded as being "father, grand-father, and great-grandfather to 147 persons".

From the northern edge of this graveyard there is a very good view of upper Longdendale, where the gritstone moors crowd in at Tintwistle and on towards Woodhead. This is perhaps the most mountainous looking defile in all the south Pennines and has the scale and proportions of real mountain country. A mile to the north of Mottram the outlier of Hollingworthhall Moor rises to 1,309 feet and separates Longdendale from the Tame Valley. Looking out from the wilder moors above Glossop, particularly Chunal Moor and Cown Edge, I have always been attracted by the look of Hollingworthhall Moor. On cold days its friendly profile, punctuated by pylons seen distantly, has been a welcoming sight after hours of travail on the high ground of highest Peakland. For various reasons the years passed without my ever reaching that little upland, but eventually I went on a bright October day, up the road from Mottram to Roe Cross, then by rutted tracks northwards across Shaw Moor. There are some wonderful vistas out to the western horizon, across Greater Manchester, from a sufficient distance to make it all seem colourful, even romantic.

Hollingworthhall Moor takes its name from Hollingworth Hall, marked until recently on One-Inch Ordnance Survey Maps in gothic-style type. Anyone walking over the moor or up the narrow lanes from Hollingworth or Roe Cross to look at this old building is sure to be disappointed because all that remains are a fine gateway, old trees, a farm and what was the stables erected in the last century. The setting is typically Pennine and protected by sycamores and beeches, but the heart has gone out of the place for the centrepiece, the Hall, is no more. The Normans realized the potential of the site, for a hunting-lodge was built here, from which base the boar and deer could be conveniently hunted in the wilderness of upper Longdendale. The Normans knew the place as 'Holisurde', and the original building was stated to be very old by 1404, then in the possession of Thomas de Holyngworthe. About 1640 the house was completely reconstructed in the contemporary Jacobean style, though the western wing seems to have been part of the much earlier building. The family, mentioned earlier in connection with the Chapel in Mottram parish church, remained here until 1734. However, some time later (early in the last century) a Captain Robert de Hollyngworth bought it, claiming to be a direct descendant of the earlier owners. Anyhow, he seems to have been an unusual man – six feet five inches tall – and to have stayed at home for most of the remainder of his life except for worship and to serve as chairman of the Hyde Bench of Magistrates. After his death in 1865 his brother sold Hollingworth Hall, and it served as a convalescent home for some years.

Then, in 1943, Manchester Corporation Waterworks purchased the property for the meagre sum of £3,100 and immediately demolished it on the grounds that drainage from the site might contaminate the Arnfield Reservoirs in the little dale some distance down the slope! I consider the wanton destruction of beautiful Hollingworth Hall to be one of the worst half dozen examples of vandalism with authority (by a so-called responsible body, too) in all this part of England. It only happened (that is, the water authority only got away with it) because the country was too busily engaged with the enemy to spare time for thought about an old building on a Pennine hill.

Certainly such desecration would not be allowed these days; but that does not bring back beautiful old Hollingworth Hall. I have seen photographs of it, the narrow courses of stone, the three storeys lit by mullioned windows, ball-topped gables and deep, stone-slated roof. Where it stood there is a sweep of rough grass, and the wind is usually moaning in the old trees which have outlived it.

Another old house, much closer to Mottram, is Mottram Old Hall. It seems to have been associated with Hollingworth Hall and was, in fact, bought by Captain Robert de Hollyngworth at about the same time that he purchased the Hollingworth dwelling. It has been much altered through the years, and what we see today is an early nineteenth-century exterior, though the stables nearby are three hundred years old. There is space here for one more outlying old building, this time on the western slopes of Harrop Edge so that it looks out of the lower Tame Valley, towards Hyde. Matley Hall Farm has an unusual courtyard, enclosed by the farmhouse ('1733' over doorway) and by buildings which were once labourers' cottages. It is stated that the old house has nineteen windows, no two alike (more a case of haphazard modification than contrived uniqueness).

To Mottram-in-Longdendale in August 1948 came one of Britain's foremost twentieth-century artists, persuaded against his better judgment by a friend who already lived there to "give it a·try". Lawrence Stephen Lowry did not like Mottram and loathed this his 'dismal' last home, which he meant to leave for many years, but he said he did not know where to go – or where he would like to go! He explained with resignation to a friend "I have no scenic sense," so it did not really matter where he laid his head at night.

Born at 8 Barrett Street, Old Trafford, Manchester on 1st November 1887, he made several moves with his family in quick succession, then settled in Rusholme, south Manchester. In 1909 they moved to 117 Station Road, Pendlebury, Salford – an industrial wasteland and something of a 'social come-down' after Rusholme. Neither L. S. Lowry nor his mother liked Pendlebury, but it was thirty-seven years before he moved again (his mother had died just prior to World War II). The new address was 72 Chorley Road, Swinton (adjacent to

Pendlebury), but in 1948 the reluctant fifteen-mile move was made to Mottram-in-Longdendale. In an interview Lowry gave to the *Manchester Evening News* in 1933, he is quoted as having said that he had "long ago decided to drop my landscape efforts" and stick to industrial scenery. He never liked the sun (he never painted shadows), and with advancing age he increasingly disliked the wet and gloomy scenery of his own district. Even so, he never left it or went abroad, largely because, as already stated, he really did not know where to go.

During World War I Lowry went watercolour painting at weekends with his young friend James Fitton. Their expeditions do not seem to have extended far beyond the urban area – to Heaton Park, Boggart Hole Clough (north-east of Manchester), Northenden (on the south bank of the Mersey west of Stockport) and Daisy Nook (between Ashton and Failsworth). His most commonly admired work is, incidentally, the fairground subject called 'Good Friday, Daisy Nook'. The pair never seem to have wandered to Pennine hill-country; it was not their sort of scenery.

Lowry's move to Mottram-in-Longdendale in 1948 was followed by the production of several 'unindustrial' landscapes, so it is perhaps correct to say that his new surroundings – the horizon of dark moorland profiles – did have some effect on his work. These landscapes include 'Agricultural Fair, Mottram-in-Longdendale' (1949), 'The House on the Moor' (1950) and 'Heathcliff's House' (1950).

Though I corresponded with this outstanding northern artist, there was no opportunity to meet him before his quite sudden death in 1976. A year later I returned to Mottram and walked from the church, down the hill and along Stalybridge Road. 'The Elms' stood drab, dark and very empty on the west side of the road. Lowry's house backs onto open fields where ponies were grazing. Beyond that the tops of the giant tower-blocks of Hattersley New Town rise as a sort of modern equivalent of his own, earlier industrial scenery. The garden was overgrown after years of semi-neglect; thistle-down was blowing in the autumn breeze.

I was informed by a short, fat man further along Stalybridge Road that souvenir-hunters were now taking pieces of Lowry's garden wall; no wonder that a complex alarm system had been installed inside 'The Elms'. Yes, he knew the artist well. He had once asked him why he always painted tall, thin people and had received the reply, "Well, you'd always draw short, fat ones, wouldn't you?"

Resting on the eastern side of Harrop Edge in the golden autumn sunlight, I could see upwards of thirty pylons striding across the hills around, cutting up the scenery. The landscape is so steep and varied, though, that it still looks good, framed between the swinging, curving wires. A mile to the north I strode over the faded heather on Hollingworthhall Moor, heather the colour of old wine blown by a soft, south wind. Mist was clinging to the far, high moors of Peakland proper; a haze which also helped to conceal part of the urban sprawl westwards to Manchester and Oldham.

18

South Pennine Waterways

The complex contours of the southern Pennines are most un-
suitable for canal construction; in fact, there are few parts of
England which presented such formidable problems to
waterway engineers two centuries ago. The geological acci-
dents which produced the South Lancashire, Yorkshire, Nottinghamshire, Derbyshire and north Staffordshire coalfields
also gave rise to important industrial conurbations separated
by high ground, difficult to traverse. Great financial incentives
drove eighteenth-century manufacturers to create the well-
remembered 'canal mania' which heralded the Canal Age.

Brilliant engineers made their names (and some of them
their fortunes) during the construction of waterways across or
near these hills. James Brindley (1716–72), William Jessop
(1745–1814) and Benjamin Outram (1764–1805) are the best
known of canal engineers responsible for waterways near the
southern Pennines.

Only three canals actually crossed the main watershed and
so connected in a direct way the lowlands on either sides of the
Pennines. The first to be completed was the Rochdale (1804);
then came the Huddersfield Narrow (1811) and finally the
Leeds and Liverpool (1816). The other waterways built adjacent to these uplands, such as the Cromford, had termini in valleys or traversed one flank, such as the Macclesfield. A glance at
a canal map of this part of England shows their reasonably even
distribution on the perimeter of the high ground, and I refer
below to each in turn, starting in the east in a clockwise direction. There are plenty of good books about British canals, and
my only reason for including this chapter is that canals, in good
repair or derelict, make excellent walking routes. In summer
the flora in and beside them is a great source of interest, likewise

the animals which inhabit them. In winter a walk beside a south Pennine canal makes an easy route below the heights when it is raining or foggy. Not least is the fascination of looking at the architecture and engineering, the industrial archæology if you like, still visible along every mile of canal.

CHESTERFIELD CANAL

Ask anyone in Chesterfield about the Chesterfield Canal and the chances are they will not know where it is, or where it goes. Such apparent ignorance or indifference is easily explained because the town's own waterway has not been operative since 1908 – the year that Norwood Tunnel (between Killamarsh and Kiveton Park) collapsed and cut off the upper twelve miles from the lower thirty-one miles, and the River Trent. Few British industrial towns are so far from the sea as Chesterfield, yet this, and the fact that high ground surrounds the district on three sides, did not prevent the planning and construction of a major waterway in the late-eighteenth century, at the commencement of the Canal Age.

The story really begins in 1769 when James Brindley was asked to make a survey by lead, coal and iron mining interests in north-east Derbyshire. By August of the same year Brindley had prepared a plan and presented it to a meeting at Worksop. It is interesting to realize that his original proposals were eventually implemented with few modifications – a canal of $45\frac{1}{2}$ miles between West Stockwith on the Trent, near Gainsborough, and Chesterfield by way of East Retford, Worksop and Staveley, with a long tunnel at the summit of the route between Kiveton Park and Killamarsh. The cost was estimated at £100,000, and Brindley conjectured an annual gross revenue of £16,400. The passing of the Chesterfield Canal Act on 28th March 1771 brought great excitement to the streets of Chesterfield, and "the utmost joy and satisfaction appeared on every countenance".

Briefly, the canal was cut westwards from the Trent at West Stockwith, across the low-lying countryside of north-eastern Nottinghamshire, through East Retford and the richly wooded landscape to Worksop. A steady climb (using thirty locks) to the broad magnesian limestone ridge at Norwood (where the

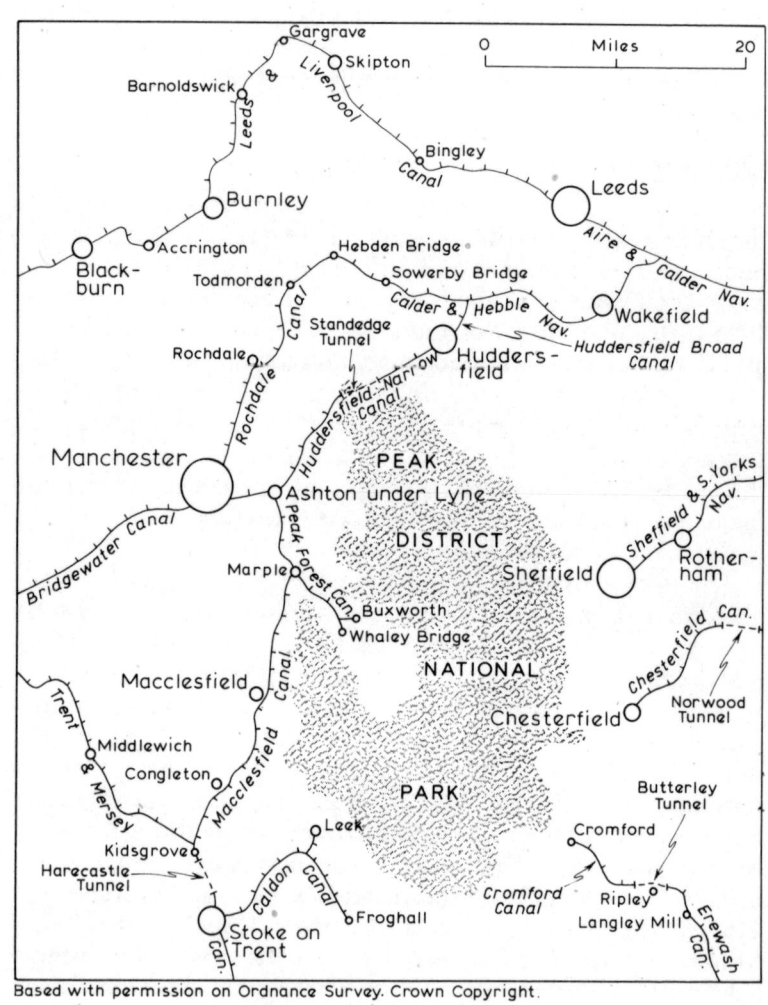

Based with permission on Ordnance Survey. Crown Copyright.

SOUTH PENNINE CANALS

tunnel saved further ascent) and so into Derbyshire and up the valley of the River Rother to Chesterfield (another nineteen locks.)

After Brindley's death in 1772, John Varley and Hugh Henshall took over control of the construction. By the spring of 1774 the central section came into service, and downstream as far as East Retford by late summer. This new communication link had an immediate beneficial effect on the townspeople of East Retford, reducing the price of coal from 15s 6d to 10s 6d per ton.

The greatest single barrier was the limestone ridge already mentioned, between the Rother Valley to the west and the Ryton Valley upstream of Worksop and Shireoaks. The solution was found in the Norwood Tunnel. In May 1775 – when it was opened to traffic – it was the longest canal tunnel in the world, measuring 1⅔ miles. The occasion was treated as something of an event, and a contemporary account records that "three vessels sailed through . . . with no less than three hundred people on board, attended with a band of music". That journey took a minute over one hour and marked a great opening-up of adjacent parts of the Derbyshire coalfield.

The Norwood Tunnel was constructed in a straight line, "being so truly directed that a person standing at one end thereof, may see out of the other". It is no longer possible easily to check the accuracy of this statement because in 1908 mining subsidence caused the collapse of the tunnel, and both entrances have long since been blocked with bricks and mortar. Since that time the almost fourteen miles of waterway between Norwood Tunnel and Chesterfield have been defunct, save for the occasional horse-drawn coal-barge which continued to use the narrowing channel into the thirties. As with most British canals, the coming of the railways in the first half of the nineteenth century dealt this waterway a shattering blow, although here the canal-owners themselves took the initiative and formed the Manchester and Lincoln Union Railway Company in 1845. One of the plans involved the conversion of the canal to a railway, part of the projected Liverpool–Great Grimsby line. The canal company was to be dissolved, but the newly-formed railway-cum-canal authority undertook to maintain the canal in "good working order, preserve its water supplies and maintain just tolls".

A multiplicity of railway companies operating in competition in this busy district of the north Derbyshire coalfield did nothing to assist the fortunes of the hard-pressed Chesterfield Canal. Revenue was £12,636 in 1848 (about the time 250,000 tons of magnesian limestone was carried by barges from quarries at Anston, near the canal between Worksop and Killamarsh, for the rebuilding of the Houses of Parliament). By 1888, though, revenue had slumped to a mere £4,734 and in 1905 the forty remaining boats were carrying only fifteen thousand tons of coal and eleven thousand tons of bricks – the major commodities at that time. During the previous thirty-four years almost continuous repairs had been necessary to maintain Norwood Tunnel in a safe condition, such were the ravages of mining subsidence. Then in 1908 came the major collapse of part of the tunnel, and this effectively sealed off the upper fourteen miles to Chesterfield. In fact, more or less all traffic was thereafter restricted between Worksop and the Trent, though coal continued to be carried from Shireoaks Colliery until 1945.

Slight commercial usage continued, but when, in 1955, the brickworks at Walkingham (three miles up from the Trent) closed, all commercial traffic ceased, and in 1962 the canal was officially abandoned. Since that time vessels have been exclusively pleasure-craft. Half a mile above Worksop Lock is Morse Lock (the fifty-ninth below Chesterfield) which marks the present official head of navigation, where a new turn-round point has been constructed. This has made the ten-mile section between East Retford and Worksop more popular with boaters.

The only part of this canal which can be fairly associated with the southern Pennines is that which winds up the Rother Valley from Norwood Tunnel to Chesterfield. Throughout most of this fourteen miles the eastern flanks of the hills can be seen some miles to the west. A walk along the old towpath, where a right of way exists, is most interesting, if only because it covers largely 'unknown' territory and provides a new viewpoint of this part of north Derbyshire. There are some surprisingly sylvan sections between the old head of navigation adjacent to Messrs Markham's Broad Oaks Works and the industrial complex at Staveley. Though largely silted up and reedy, the towpath remains fairly firm and excavation of the canal would not be an insuperable problem.

Beyond Staveley the canal is reduced to a small drainage ditch in an area opencast for coal some years ago; then at Renishaw a steel works' slag heap obscures it altogether. At Killamarsh two or three new houses on a small private development have been erected on the line of the waterway, and at the time of writing (1978) there is talk of these houses having to be demolished because the local council gave permission for their construction without any thought for the diversion of what is, after all, a public right of way. Thereafter the canal resumes something of its original character, overhung with hawthorn and alder, and there are broad views down the Rother Valley towards Rotherham.

Then comes Norwood Bottom Lock with its broad pool, footbridge and the attractive white-washed dwelling which was until 1909 a public house; this marks the bottom of the flight of thirteen locks which carried vessels up the slope to the western portal of Norwood Tunnel, one mile distant. It is certainly one of the steepest flights of locks in Britain.

At the bricked-up tunnel mouth, just below the constant roar of the M1 motorway, the part of the Chesterfield Canal which concerns us here comes to an end, though one may pass beneath the motorway and walk on the line of the tunnel to the eastern portal and so through delightful, wooded country by Turnerwood to Shireoaks and Worksop.

What of the future? The Chesterfield Canal Society was formed in 1976 "to further the protection, conservation and restoration of the Chesterfield Canal and to advocate the fullest appropriate use by all interests of the whole canal and its environs". The long-term aim for the forgotten fourteen miles above Norwood Tunnel is to provide a linear recreational spine for ramblers, anglers and naturalists in an area singularly lacking in water space. It is hoped that over the years the mid-section between Norwood Tunnel and Worksop can be restored to full navigational standard – a very costly project, of course, involving the rebuilding of many locks. One wonders if such plans have any chance of success in this world of rising costs and whether – as so often happens – the present genteel, sylvan decay of sections such as that about Thorpe and Turnerwood Locks would be destroyed by restoration and inevitably increased usage by the dense population of surrounding districts. The little known reaches of this once busy waterway are at present a true Aladdin's Cave for the pedestrian who comes upon the scene unawares.

CROMFORD CANAL

With the opening of the Erewash Canal in 1779, Langley Mill and adjacent districts of the Nottinghamshire and Derbyshire coalfield became linked with the Trent, and a tide of industrial expansion rose up the Erewash Valley. It was only nine years later that industrialists and other interested parties met to discuss the possibility of extending this canal beyond Langley Mill, to provide cheap transport for coal, iron and carboniferous limestone. There was even a suggestion of making some sort of trading link with Manchester across the watershed of the southern Pennines.

The necessary Act of Parliament was passed in 1789 and William Jessop and Benjamin Outram were made responsible for the engineering. The resulting Cromford Canal was completed by 1794 and wound up the Erewash Valley from Langley Mill, turning westwards to Ripley, along the lower reaches of the Amber Valley to Ambergate and thence northwards for five miles to Cromford. Here were Sir Richard Arkwright's cotton mills, just beside the head of navigation, which benefited greatly after 1794 from the presence of such convenient transportation. In reciprocation the canal received water at the terminal wharf direct from the cottonmills.

The Cromford was a successful business venture, and by 1841–2 goods traffic had risen to 320,000 tons. There was even a privately operated passenger service between Cromford and Nottingham for many years, vessels using the now derelict Nottingham Canal beyond Langley Mill. In the early years of the nineteenth century there had been a plan to extend the canal beyond Cromford, via Bakewell and the upper Wye Valley to join the Peak Forest Canal at Buxworth, near Chinley and so give a through route from the Trent to the Mersey. The engineering problems involved caused this proposal to be dropped and instead the Cromford and High Peak Railway was constructed and opened in 1831. The engineer was William Jessop's son, Josiah. The railway left the canal one mile south of Cromford, at the place which came to be known as High Peak Wharf. Here goods were transferred between waterway and railway. The thirty-three-mile-long line crosses the limestone plateau and reaches 1,264 feet above sea level south-east of Buxton. This line descended into the Goyt Valley to link up with the Peak Forest Canal at Whaley Bridge.

Competition from railways affected this canal after 1850, and when the Midland Railway purchased it in 1870, there was only a little local traffic using it. As with the Chesterfield Canal, the Cromford had a long tunnel on its middle section, the three-thousand-yards-long Butterley Tunnel passing underneath Ripley. After several roof collapses towards the end of the century, it was finally closed by a serious collapse in 1900. Thereafter the upper half, between Butterley Tunnel and Cromford, was used by a little local traffic, but the entire waterway was finally abandoned in 1944. Since that time the lower section between Butterley and Langley Mill has become utterly ruinous, and most of it in the Erewash Valley has been filled in altogether.

Ironically it is the five miles at the head of this navigation which remains in the best condition. The Cromford Canal Society was formed in 1971 to protect and preserve that five-mile section. In 1974 its ownership was transferred from the British Waterways Board to Derbyshire County Council, and the Canal Society has undertaken to care for it. Much restoration work has already taken place at Cromford Wharf and a mile to the south at High Peak Wharf, where goods were formerly transferred between canal and railway. Immediately south of this are two of the most interesting features of the Cromford Canal – the imposing Leawood Pump of 1849 which could raise twenty-four tons of water from the adjacent River Derwent to the canal every minute using steam power, and William Jessop's single-span Wigwell Aqueduct over the Derwent which collapsed soon after construction and had to be rebuilt more massively.

In the summer months a horse-drawn boat, *John Gray*, operates at week-ends between Cromford Wharf and Lea Pump. The Society anticipates that the remaining section, from the Lea

Pump to Ambergate, will receive necessary maintenance work and that it will be regarded principally as a nature reserve.

CALDON CANAL

This waterway is, strictly speaking, a branch of the Trent and Mersey Canal, from which it runs at Etruria, Stoke-on-Trent, for 17½ miles into the glorious Churnet Valley as far as Froghall. It was opened to traffic in 1779, and a short branch to Leek was added in 1802. At the same time an extension was built from Froghall, down the Churnet Valley to Uttoxeter, but this was closed before 1850 and part of the route converted to the Macclesfield–Uttoxeter line of the North Staffordshire Railway (later part of the LMSR system).

One of the interesting facts about the Caldon Canal is that while the section from Hazelhurst Junction (where the Leek Branch forks) to Froghall (eight miles) remained a statutory waterway, it was inaccessible after 1961 because stop-planks were inserted because the Hazelhurst Top Lock gate was considered unsafe; at the same time the Leek Branch had been formally abandoned in 1944 but remained navigable because it was retained as a 'navigable feeder' – carrying water to the lower section of the Caldon and so to the summit of the Trent and Mersey at Etruria. Most of this water comes from Rudyard Reservoir, two miles beyond the Leek Branch terminus.

Most of the Caldon's length is through delightfully unspoilt country, typically north Staffordshire farmland with steep valleys, woodland and far views of toppled hills. This is the western edge of the southermost Pennines. Only the first mile or two from Etruria is really industrialized, and that makes an interesting contrast with the pastorale which follows as we walk or glide towards the hills.

During the seventies the Caldon Canal has had much loving care and attention paid to it, and now it is again navigable right along the Churnet Valley to Froghall amid the little hills and hanging woods where the limestone country begins.

MACCLESFIELD CANAL

This waterway traverses the western fringe of the Peak District for twenty-six miles from the Trent and Mersey Canal at Kidsgrove to the Peak Forest Canal at Marple, Cheshire. It was the last of the waterways mentioned here to be constructed, opening to traffic in 1831, and passes for almost its entire length through attractive countryside. It was designed by Thomas Telford.

The walk along its towpath makes a good day's expedition and offers broad views out to the west across the Cheshire Plain. The hills are apparent to the east for the entire journey – Mow Cop, The Cloud, Gawsworth Common, Kerridge Hill, Nab Head and the moorlands about Lyme Park. The canal is very popular with pleasure-craft users as it forms one arm of the noted Cheshire Canal Ring.

An interesting feature of the Macclesfield is the number of beautiful accommodation bridges of local stone, some with curved ramps to enable the boat-horse to cross to the other bank without being disconnected. Here and there are white-painted swing bridges (as at Oakgrove, south of Macclesfield) which must be opened and closed by the boat crew.

Between Macclesfield and Congleton the canal descends 110 feet in one mile as it goes southwards. This is achieved with the twelve Bosley locks, and south of these again, where the canal turns westwards for a couple of miles, there is an airy aqueduct high over the River Dane where that river flows out of the hills and on towards the plain.

Almost eight miles north of Macclesfield the canal flows under an arched towpath bridge and meets the Peak Forest Canal here at Marple.

PEAK FOREST CANAL

Opened at the commencement of the nineteenth century, this $14\frac{1}{2}$-mile waterway was built between Dukinfield Junction on the Ashton Canal at the heart of an industrial area bordering eastern Manchester and the Buxworth Basin, near Whaley Bridge. The Ashton Canal runs westwards from Dukinfield Junction into central Manchester, while the Macclesfield Canal branches south-westwards from the Peak Forest at Marple, seven miles south of Dukinfield Junction.

The Ashton, the Peak Forest and the Macclesfield have long

been closely associated and were, in fact, the property of one ownership before waterways were nationalized in January 1948. The Cromford and High Peak Railway already referred to crossed the Peak District watershed north-westwards from the Cromford Canal and came down to Whaley Bridge, where a half-mile branch from near Buxworth had its terminus at an interesting warehouse which now houses a small museum. In this terminal building goods and passengers were transferred between canal and railway.

The Peak Forest Tramway carried limestone down to the Buxworth Basin from Dove Holes Quarry between 1799 and 1926, after which the basin became derelict and has only recently been restored by the efforts of the Inland Waterways Protection Society. A walk along the length of the canal from Whaley Bridge to Dukinfield Junction makes a rewarding day's outing, and there are trains back to Whaley Bridge from Guide Bridge, a mile from Dukinfield Junction.

I think the most interesting section of the canal is that from the junction with the Macclesfield Canal at Marple, northwards for three miles to Romiley. First comes the series of sixteen locks in quick succession which carry the waterway 210 feet down to the famous Marple Aqueduct. Incidentally, the section between the top lock at Marple and the terminus at Whaley Bridge is at five hundred feet above sea level, the highest navigation open to traffic in Britain today. Anyway, having gone down by the Marple locks, one comes under the shading trees to the crossing of the Goyt Valley. The Marple Aqueduct was designed by Benjamin Outram and a local engineer, Thomas Brown. The three arches carry the canal at more than a hundred feet above the River Goyt, but to get a good view of it one must go down through the trees to the valley floor. Opened in 1800, it is one of the best looking aqueducts in the country.

The scenery becomes increasingly urban beyond Romiley. Woodley is followed by Hyde and Newton Wood, then Dukinfield. A fine stone warehouse of 1834 stood at the junction of the Peak Forest and Ashton Canal at Dukinfield, but this was destroyed by fire in 1972. While the Ashton Canal (opened in 1799) goes westwards towards Manchester, the third arm goes eastwards towards the Pennines. This third arm is the Huddersfield Narrow Canal.

HUDDERSFIELD NARROW CANAL

Of all the waterways of the region, I consider this the most Pennine. It goes closest to the high gritstone moors, and anyone following its course is in sight of the hills for most of the twenty-mile journey.

Opened in 1811, it linked the Yorkshire and Lancashire canal systems, crossing the Pennine watershed through the Standedge Tunnel – at 5,698 yards, the longest canal tunnel ever constructed. The engineer was Benjamin Outram, and the canal joins the Peak Forest and the Ashton at Dukinfield Junction. It follows the Tame Valley north-north-eastwards for nine miles to Diggle before entering Standedge Tunnel. Beyond that it goes down the Colne Valley through Marsden and Slaithwaite to join the Huddersfield Broad Canal at Huddersfield.

The walk along the line of the canal (and over Standedge following the course of the tunnel by the prominent air-shafts) makes a rewarding twenty-mile excursion.

Closed in 1944, the Huddersfield Narrow had seventy-four narrow locks, but many of these have long since gone. In fact, sections of the waterway are completely ruinous. At Stalybridge its line has been built over, and one must aim through several streets without any tangible evidence of it and hope to find it again on the far side. The hills come crowding in as one walks on up the Tame Valley, through Mossley and Saddleworth; then in a semi-wild gritstone basin at Diggle the canal enters Standedge Tunnel through locked gates.

The boat journey through three miles of darkness is famous in the anals of canal lore. Close beside it is Standedge railway tunnel, and at intervals along the bore the boater was reminded of the River Styx, for adits connecting the tunnels (the canal bore acts as a drain for the railway bore) allowed sight, sound and smell of trains to reach the canal. In the days of steam haulage, choking smoke drifted through the connecting adits, and flying sparks and the glint from the firebox must have been enough to convince many that they had indeed reached the gates of Hades.

The Standedge canal tunnel took seventeen years to complete and cost £160,000. Its south-western portal is close beside the Manchester-Huddersfield railway route at Diggle, near the head of that bleak hollow which is overlooked by Castle Shaw Roman fort to the north-west and the Pennine watershed (where the Pennine Way runs) to the east. Beyond the tunnel the Huddersfield Narrow Canal passes down the narrow confines of the Colne Valley, a semi-industrialized valley punctuated by old mill buildings and tall chimneys, and always the steep hills around as you walk on towards the town.

ROCHDALE CANAL

This canal, too, crossed the main watershed of the Pennines between Manchester and Sowerby Bridge (at the head of Yorkshire's Calder and Hebble Navigation). Unlike the Huddersfield Narrow, no long tunnel was needed on its original thirty-three-mile course; instead no fewer than ninety-two locks were required to carry the Rochdale northwards to Rochdale then up the valley of the River Roch and over to Todmorden and down the Calder Valley by way of Hebden Bridge to Sowerby Bridge.

Completed in 1804, the Rochdale Canal last saw commercial traffic in 1937 and was officially abandoned in 1952. Most of its length is now derelict, but the towpath makes an interesting walking route, especially in the hill country between Littleborough and Sowerby Bridge. Only two miles of this waterway are still open, forming a vital link in the Cheshire Waterways Ring, between the Ashton Canal and the Bridgewater Canal in central Manchester.

LEEDS AND LIVERPOOL CANAL

The last of the three trans-Pennine canals to be completed, in 1816, it measures 127 miles and is still fully navigable. The initial twenty-eight miles from Liverpool were completed in 1775, and the $33\frac{1}{2}$ miles from Leeds to Gargrave were finished in 1777. Nevertheless the difficult terrain south-westwards from Gargrave, by Barnoldswick, Nelson and Burnley and on by Accrington to Blackburn took years more to cross.

It can fairly be said that the line of this waterway between Leeds, Skipton and Burnley marks the northern extremity of the southern Pennines. Beyond it, including Pendle Hill and the limestone country of the upper Aire Valley, we are really in the central Pennines.

Though I have never sailed or walked the length of the Leeds and Liverpool, such a thing would make a fascinating expedition, for it crosses many types of landscape and a whole range of industrial scenery, from Lancashire cotton conurbations to West Yorkshire woollen towns, culminating in Leeds at the eastern limit of the waterway.

CALDER AND HEBBLE NAVIGATION

Growing industrialization in the second half of the eighteenth century encouraged canal development up the Calder Valley west of Wakefield. By 1770 the Calder and Hebble Navigation had been engineered as far as Sowerby Bridge, and this proved to be the farthest development of the canal into the Pennines. However, thirty years later the Rochdale Canal came down the upper Calder Valley, through Hebden Bridge and Mytholmroyd, to link up with the Calder and Hebble at Sowerby Bridge. Since the demise of the Rochdale, that canal has been piped underground at Sowerby Bridge, so there is no chance of boating from one to the other.

The Calder Navigation Society was formed in 1968 and has as its major purpose the development of the amenities of the canal for walkers, anglers and boating enthusiasts. The $21\frac{1}{2}$ miles between Wakefield and Sowerby Bridge are largely industrial, or within sight of urban scenery, but there are some attractive reaches, as, for example, in the vicinity of Long Lees Lock, near Elland.

HUDDERSFIELD BROAD CANAL

This $3\frac{1}{4}$-mile-long waterway is also known as 'Sir John Ramsden's Canal' and can really be thought of as a branch of the Calder & Hebble Navigation, from which it forks at Cooper Bridge, between Mirfield and Brighouse. It was finished in 1776 and was linked with the Huddersfield Narrow Canal when the latter was completed in 1811 to make a trans-Pennine route between Manchester and the West Riding.

The canal with its nine wide-beam locks is still fully navigable up to the Aspley Basin in Huddersfield, now a popular boating mecca known as Aspley Marina.

SHEFFIELD AND SOUTH YORKSHIRE NAVIGATION

This forty-three-mile-long system of canals extends from the Trent at Keadby, north of Gainsborough, to the dark, industrial centre of Sheffield, and it is only the upper few miles which can really claim to have any place in this chapter. This navigation was formed in 1895 from several separate waterways, the uppermost of which was the Sheffield Canal (opened to traffic in 1819). This early-nineteenth-century canal connects Sheffield with the Don Navigation (operating by 1751) at Tinsley, a distance of only three miles or so.

Unlike the other canals described above, the Sheffield Canal is utterly urban, and generally satanic. Despoiled by chemical and general industrial pollution and by dumps of rubbish, this makes a good subject for a short walk on a wet winter's day – to see the utter desolation wrought by man in his quest for material wealth. Even so, the decaying Victorian warehouses around the Sheffield terminal basin have architectural merit, and most of this end of the canal is now listed as worthy of preservation. I have seen it stated that this could be "the most exciting canal basin in Britain", but much time, money and effort will have to be spent if this ideal is ever to be realized.

During the summer of 1978 a plan was put forward by British Waterways Board, South Yorkshire County Council and local industrialists to spend £8 million on modernizing the Sheffield and South Yorkshire Navigation. It has been stated that "the only strong runner among British canals which pretend to a commercial future" is this particular canal. It will be interesting to see what the future holds for this navigation.

19

Exploring Cheshire's River Dean

The little River Dean is a child of the south Pennines, a wild, upland stream which flows down westwards and onto the Cheshire Plain at Bollington. It continues its journey north-westwards for almost another nine miles to join the larger River Bollin near Wilmslow, a total distance from source of less than fourteen miles. Within that short space this little-known water travels some exceedingly attractive country, from wild gritstone steeps near the Derbyshire border to fertile, green pastures and the fringe of Greater Manchester's southern suburbs in central-northern Cheshire.

To follow its course, or approximately so, would make an interesting day's walk, emphasizing the great contrasts found in England within a small compass, nowhere greater than on the flanks of the Pennines.

The source of the River Dean lies near Longclough, half a mile due west of Shining Tor (1,834 feet) which is the highest point in Cheshire since local government re-organization in 1974. Actually the summit is shared with Derbyshire, as the county boundary traverses this lofty watershed separating Buxton and Macclesfield near the famous Cat and Fiddle Inn, second highest public house in England.

The initial $4\frac{1}{2}$ miles in the Dean's young life are through or, more accurately, down the western flanks of the gritstone uplands which form part of the Peak District National Park. The upper three miles of its course are within this Park. Much of this brown upland is, typically, an area of rural de-population, with gaunt farms such as Thursbitch and Eaves now ruins inhabited only by sheltering sheep and picnicking ramblers taking shelter from wind, rain or snow. These western slopes are crossed by a network of minor hill roads which make access relatively easy, even to fairly remote corners such as pretty Jenkin Chapel sheltered by a handful of wind-bent syca-mores and quite like a setting for a Brontë novel. In bright weather, though, these Cheshire heights smile and present ideal territory for walking.

Despite relative remoteness, there have been changes in the upper valley of the Dean. The narrow hill road that twists southwards from Jenkin Chapel comes, in a mile, to derelict Hooleyhey Farm, and there, below the buildings, is the new Lamaload Reservoir. An attractive and fairly inconspicuous concrete dam impounds the Dean, and this artificial lake un-doubtedly adds a new element to the hill scenery hereabouts. There are several footpaths to cross the slopes near the reser-voir, and one of the best goes by Lower Ballgreave to the Setter Dog Inn at Walker Barn on the Buxton-Macclesfield road.

Below Lamaload the river flows through the pretty upland village of Rainow, clinging to both sides of the old hill road join-ing Whaley Bridge and Macclesfield. A narrow, steep-sided ridge turns the Dean northwards beyond Rainow, a finger of high ground which attains 1,028 feet called Kerridge Hill. Composed of good quality gritstone, Kerridge has been exten-sively quarried on its western flanks though the scars are now well weathered and the old rock faces add an attractive extra feature. The best-known feature here, though, is 'White Nancy' at the 920-feet-high northern end of the ridge. This takes the form of a tall, whitewashed structure shaped like an old straw bee-hive. Many visitors must have wondered about the history of White Nancy.

An ordnance beacon of brick apparently stood here before 1810, and in a local history of the Macclesfield district (pub-lished 1825) it is stated that a Mr Gaskell of Rainow built "a round building, clothed in white, called Northern Nancy". The name 'Nancy' probably came from the several females of the Gaskell family who had that Christian name. Another point is that the leading horse used to drag the slab of stone which formed the seat within the building was called Nancy, possibly after those same ladies.

During the thirties the structure was described as being in a "much broken" condition. In a local newspaper article it was asked if it was beyond "the wit of man to devise ways and means of keeping this place in repair". The answer seems to have been to seal the structure completely, rendering it with a smooth coat of concrete and painting it brilliant white – and so it remains, except for a rash (but not unattractive one) of writing in pencil and paint spray. In clear weather shipping is visible on the Mersey.

White Nancy still looks down from her ridge-end belvedere to "her Bollington admirers in the Happy Valley below". Bollington is a little industrial town of once-prosperous silk and cotton mills beside the River Dean, not, as one would expect, the larger River Bollin which flows out across the plain two miles to the west. A more important waterway here is the Macclesfield Canal which winds northwards from Macclesfield, through Bollington and on by Marple to join the Peak Forest Canal near Stockport. This was once a vital link with the town, bringing raw materials to the mills and taking away the finished textiles. Now it is a quiet backwater, used mainly by holiday craft.

Here at Bollington the Dean is joined by its major tributary, the Harrop Brook, which flows down from the high ground to the east. The headwaters of this stream are quite close to 1,150 feet near lonely, hill-top Blue Boar Farm. Down into the little side-valley comes the Harrop Brook and passes not far from the extremely steep hillside of Brink Brow where motorcycle hill-climbs have been held for many years. I well remember a cold winter Sunday when the Manchester 17 Club were holding their meeting. I had motorcycled over the hills from the east and enjoyed an afternoon in the bitter wind at the foot of the hill. The air was filled with the exotic aroma of vegetable racing-oil as Triumphs, BSAs and Nortons roared up Brink Brow, towards the grey clouds and the mass of faces silhouetted there. Brink Brow remains but those long-lived British marques have gone to their long rest.

Less than three miles below its quiet source, the Harrop Brook is joined by a stream draining from the north. In its little valley lies Pott Shrigley, one of the most attractive villages in all this south Pennine country. It stands amid high trees and steep, patchwork slopes, and the unusual name is derived from the words 'shriggel' – a wood frequented by 'shrikes' – and 'pott' – 'a pool', though Pott is also a local family name so the actual origin is something of an enigma – 'Pott's wood where shrikes are common' perhaps?

The outstanding architectural feature of the village is definitely the tower of St Christopher's church. The whole building is unusual because it is mainly constructed of millstone grit, and that is rare for a Cheshire church; more particularly, its tower is very large for such a modest building. It would do credit to a much bigger town church, with its beautiful pinnacles and battlements framed by mature deciduous trees. There was a chantry chapel here from 1498, but an older building definitely stood on the site, and the very tall cross in the graveyard was probably the original preaching cross once so common and from which the early priests conducted their services.

Below Bollington the River Dean is a lowland water, winding ever more sinuously across the fertile Cheshire Plain. There are no important towns along the way, only an occasional farmhouse and hamlet. The most interesting spot in this lower half of the Dean's territory is Adlington, three miles below Bollington. Here, on the site of a pre-Norman hunting lodge, stands beautiful Adlington Hall. The Legh family have lived here for six centuries, and the house has been altered and enlarged several times. It is now cared for by the National Trust, and the approach from the lane skirting the northern side of the park brings one past the impressive stable block (now serving as luxury flats) and out under mature trees to the black-and-white east front of the house.

Adlington Hall was once moated – the remains of this are still visible – and the oldest part of the house is one of Cheshire's best half-timbered buildings. At the centre of the house is a courtyard, from which one gets a good impression of the Elizabethan half-timbering and the red brickwork dating from the alterations of 1757. The house is open to visitors during the summer, and one of the most interesting internal features to be seen is the three-hundred-year-old Smith organ on which, traditionally, Handel composed his 'Harmonious Blacksmith' while staying at Adlington.

Two miles due south of Adlington is the village of Prestbury, on the banks of the River Bollin. Now, I was surprised when I first walked through this settlement, surprised by its neatness and its obvious present affluence. Perhaps it is attractive, but in a rather artificial, twee sort of way – a suburb of Macclesfield and Manchester. It is a dormitory village of the type we associate more with the wealthier parts of Surrey or Kent and not especially with the lowland fringe of the southern Pennines.

Prestbury means 'priests' fort', and the remains of a Saxon cross and a Norman chapel in the churchyard of St Peter's suggests a centre of worship here since perhaps the fifth century. In fact, this relatively small village commanded an extensive parish which included Macclesfield and Bollington in the Middle Ages. Millward and Robinson have recently pointed out that Bollington developed as a series of scattered smallholdings on the fringe of Prestbury. The passage of time has reversed these roles: the development of industry and the Macclesfield Canal enlarged Bollington, for instance, so that in 1834 it achieved the status of an independent parish. Prestbury is many people's dream of an ideal place to live and has retained its railway station on the main line between Macclesfield and Manchester while busy Bollington has lost its railway link.

The River Dean flows gently north-westwards beyond Adlington, across a broad plain dotted with dairy farms and enhanced by tall trees. In one and a half miles it flows under the Stockport–Wilmslow road at the place called Deanwater, near Dean Farm and Dean Row.

Now the river meanders greatly, between Handforth and Wilmslow. Here the valley narrows and is wooded – then it passes beneath the lane to Styal and immediately joins the larger River Bollin which, in turn, continues for a further twelve miles to the Mersey upstream of Warrington. At Styal, near the mouth of the Dean, the old cotton-mill remains by the Bollin, and nearby is the neo-Elizabethan Norcliffe Hall where the great American ornithologist Audubon stayed with the wealthy Gregs. Many of the attractive buildings at Styal, some of them typically half-timbered, are in the care of the National Trust and are well worth a detour from the major highway to examine at leisure.

20

The Dane Valley

The Dane Valley is one of those places impossible to appreciate unless on foot, a beautiful upland valley in the gritstone of western Peakland with a very particular character. I tend to think of it as a miniature of the upper reaches of Swaledale, for its narrow confines are not really like any other valley of the region.

The source of the Dane lies at 1,650 feet on the gently shelving heather moor at Whetstone Ridge, less than one mile south of the Cat and Fiddle Inn beside the Buxton–Macclesfield road. Almost immediately the peaty stream becomes the boundary between Cheshire and Derbyshire. After a couple of miles, at the Panniers Pool Bridge, the river becomes the frontier between Cheshire and Staffordshire and continues as such until it leaves the hills. For all those ten miles from moor-top source to plain level the Dane courses through a beautiful area of steep slopes and hidden bowers and maintains an atmosphere all its own. This characteristic charm is compounded of the unique topographical shapes and the gritstone forming them; also responsible is the pattern of hill farming and the unchanging countenance of ancient habitations; not least, too, the old place names which blend so well with this locality.

There are shooting-butts still in use in late summer and autumn on the high ground where the Dane rises. In the uppermost reaches of the valley proper are the remains of Danebower and Reeve Edge Quarries, where gritstone was once won for building material. I remember, on a summer day of long ago, exploring the crumpled ground of Reeve Edge Quarries with my parents, strictly private then though long since closed down, when we saw a tweed-clad figure striding purposefully across the moor in our direction. Who he was we did not know, but we made good our escape, back across the Dane and up by Danebower Colliery to the Buxton road. The distant figure was last seen scratching his head in that toppled wilderness of gritstone heaps.

Mention of Danebower Colliery reminds me that there was much sporadic coal-mining hereabouts in the nineteenth century, and this particular working on the slope directly to the south of the Buxton–Congleton road still has its blunt chimney intact, a singularly attractive memorial to this isolated pocket of Victorian industry. Sheep pens stand below the chimney, close beside the infant Dane. The river curves on down near Holt and Sparbent Farms and then passes under Panniers Pool Bridge where the three counties meet. This spot is traditionally associated with the medieval courts summoned to hear evidence against trespassers in the medieval Macclesfield Forest. This preserve, like the Royal Forest of the Peak, was held strictly in the grip of the forest laws and stretched as far south as Bosley, where the Dane winds out of the hills and enters the plain, and northwards to Marple. Here, at the Panniers Poolside, in more recent times the notorious Flash coiners had secret gatherings.

Below Three Shire Heads (at Panniers Pool) the little Dane trickles on down gritstone steps for a couple of miles to Gradbach. Here is the amazing gorge cut by the Dane through the enclosing gritstone edges rimming the Roaches Basin, an important geological syncline (or downfold). It seems that at one time the river flowed at a much higher level, and rapid downcutting through the sandstones and soft shales has created this gorge, now well wooded in parts. Where the Black Brook swerves down from the east and joins the Dane below Gradbach, there is a particularly beautiful hanging wood on the southern slopes; it is part of Back Forest. Up here is the mysterious and romantic Lud's Church – but more of that soon.

Gradbach is a scattered area of farms, cottages and the remains of early industry. The fast water of the Dane attracted mill-builders to this part of the valley. Gradbach Mill was built in 1640, but it is uncertain what was produced here for the first 140 years. However, in 1780 the Dakeyne family purchased the mill, and for a century they manufactured sewing-silk and did some weaving. In 1785 the mill was destroyed by fire, but the

Dakeynes soon had it rebuilt. About 1885 it was sold to Sir John Harpur Crewe of Calke Abbey, south of Derby. The mill was thereafter used for sawing timber. For many years now Gradbach Mill has lain empty and derelict. In his informative book *Dane Valley Story* (1953), Clifford Rathbone claimed that the thirty-eight-foot water-wheel of this mill was the largest pocket water-wheel remaining in England. Each of its ninety-six water pockets had a capacity of thirty-five gallons, and through its gearing one revolution of the giant wheel caused the driving shaft inside the building to revolve 2,500 times. All this gearing, the shafting and the wheel have gone, but the overgrown water channel remains where the Dane water ran down towards the mill and did its pollution-free work before rejoining the main stream.

The interesting old farmhouse beside the road at Burntcliff Top, to the north of Gradbach Mill, was until 1919 the Eagle and Child Inn, taking its name from the crest of the Stanleys, Earls of Derby, who are lords of this manor. On 10th August 1884 it is recorded that the local Shepherd's Club held its annual feast here. A fife and drum band led a procession down the lane to Allgreave Chapel for a service, and the company then returned to Burntcliff Top for the feast and games.

When silk thread was produced at Gradbach in the eighteenth and nineteenth centuries, when the Dane Valley was experiencing its industrial heyday, it is recorded that there were fifty or so cottages in the neighbourhood, which have since completely vanished from the landscape. The power of the river was superseded by the power of steam and this remote location made transport expensive so the workers drifted to the towns on the edge of the plain, to Leek and Congleton and Macclesfield. A dwindling agricultural population has further eroded the population so that the Methodist Chapel at Gradbach Bridge (upstream of the silk mill), which held its first service at Easter 1849, is now closed, along with the village school.

In the days of the last Dakeynes to own Gradbach Mill, prior to 1885, the single-storey addition was built onto the Mill House, adjacent to the Mill. These Dakeynes were doctors, and the addition served as a surgery for them. In the inter-war years – the days of the great swing to rambling – this low building was a café. More recently several crystal streams on the hillside near the Mill have provided the mineral-rich water for a thriving watercress business. Clifford Rathbone relates that Joseph Sigley of the Mill House was the only person in the country who had a market stall exclusively for the sale of watercress (at Macclesfield).

Below the confluence of the Black Brook with the Dane rise the hanging woods already mentioned. Up here is the site of a remarkable landslip called Lud's Church. In strictly geomorphological terms, this splitting of the surface resulted from a slipping of the sandstone of the upper slopes. It was probably first recorded in print in the seventeenth century, when the Staffordshire historian Dr Plot described its narrow confines as capable of holding snow all the summer through – one enterprising Quarnford man emptied a sackful of old snow taken from Lud's Church onto the market square at Leek on 17th July three centuries ago.

During the fourteenth and fifteenth centuries the immediate followers of Wycliffe, the 'Lollards', sought refuge from the ecclesiastical authorities in this remote district. Their pastor-leader was the illustrious Walter de Lud-auk, and on one occasion about 1405 fourteen Lollards were worshipping here at Lud's Church – an ideal hideout for their services – when they were surprised by soldiers out searching for them. The lovely Alice, Walter's granddaughter, was mortally wounded in the struggle and the rest of the congregation surrendered and were taken away. Walter de Lud-auk died in London, a prisoner in chains far from the quiet hills where he had been relatively free to follow the uninhibited, reformed ideals of Wycliffe. Lud's Church is still a secret sort of cleft, much of it draped with mosses and lichens which give a peculiar, almost unique, lighting effect. Visitors came from far places in Victorian times to see this chasm and its magic light; then the visitors seemed to die away, and for many years Lud's Church was almost left to its own devices. In very recent years the number of people seeking it out has greatly increased, and the padding of countless feet on the floor of the ravine and up its walls is at last having a damaging effect on the vegetation. The church is ever so subtly having its curtains of green – and, therefore, its singular light – destroyed by unintentional wear and tear. As so often happens in a marvellous and natural place, the source of interest is causing its own destruction by attracting too much attention in a massively over-populated island such as ours.

The Dane flows on westwards below Lud's Church and is soon joined by the Clough Brook draining Wildboarclough. This latter dale is dominated by Peakland's most shapely hill – Shutlingsloe (1,659 feet), literally 'Scyttel's hill' – which is capped by a bed of hard gritstone tilting at about thirty degrees towards the west and from which there are some of the best views in this part of England – as far as the estuary of the Mersey in clear conditions.

Below the confluence with the Clough Brook, the Dane Valley winds on to the south-west, bordered now by thick and attractive woodland. Up on the slope to the west of the valley is the village of Wincle. The ancient route between Cleulow Cross and Heaton goes steeply down from Wincle to cross the Dane at, appropriately, Danebridge. On the steep hill below Wincle church stands the sixteenth-century Ship Inn with its hand-painted sign depicting Sir Ernest Shackleton's vessel *Nimrod*. Across the valley from Wincle stands Swythamley Hall, former home of the late Sir Philip Brocklehurst, who was a member of Shackleton's British Antarctic Expedition of 1907 and one of the party which made the first ascent of Mount Erebus on Ross Island in 1908. For his work in the Antarctic Sir Philip received the Polar Medal and clasp of the Royal Geographical Society and became a Fellow of that Society in 1915. At Eton and Cambridge he had a considerable reputation as an athlete, gaining a boxing Blue and later became a well-known horseman. He was wounded in the Great War and later became attached to the Egyptian Army, returning to the Middle East early in the last war as an officer commanding the 2nd Regiment Arab Legion Desert Mechanized Brigade. He died quite recently, a bachelor, aged eighty-seven, and now his extensive estate at Swythamley, across the Dane in Staffordshire, has been sold. At one time there was a considerable collection of exotic animals in Swythamley Park, and tales have been told of climbers on the nearby Roaches reaching the top of that escarpment to come face to face with a yak or a brown bear. The wallabies which escaped from the Park years ago have found life in this quarter of Peakland singularly amenable, and they still inhabit remote corners of the moors, rarely seen by man. One adventurous wallaby left its footprints in the snow at Bull Close Farm above the Drone Valley of north-east Derbyshire some years ago but was later killed by a train in the valley below.

A very interesting (now rare) book about this part of the Dane Valley is Brocklehurst's *Swythamley and its Neighbourhood*, published by Hardwicke in 1874. The painting of the *Nimrod* at the Ship Inn, Wincle was commissioned by Sir Philip Brocklehurst's mother as a memory of her son's Antarctic adventures.

Downstream of Danebridge, directly below the Ship Inn, the valley is deep-cut and sinuous. It is well wooded, and there are only limited views through the trees. From clearings near Bearda Farm one can look to the north-west across the Dane Valley to the open hills of Wincle Minn and Bosley Minn; funny names these, and with a most clear and interesting history. The important Cistercian abbey at Combermere in south-western Cheshire gained a gift of land in the twelfth century from the Earl of Chester. It was in Macclesfield Forest, "in a place which is called Winchul", and was for the erection of a grange (or outlying farm) and consisted of pasturage for two thousand sheep, their lambs, twenty-four cows, two bulls and an assemblage of draught animals (oxen and horses). Old records show that wool from the Combermere estate went via Boston to Flanders.

Millward and Robinson have quite recently pointed out the almost unique character of Wincle Grange, still remote on its unseen hillside above the Dane at nine hundred feet. The building seen today was erected in the fifteenth century, with additions, and is certainly one of the oldest and least altered dwellings in the south Pennines. It owes much of this lack of disturbance to the remote position, unseen by most folk on this, the 'wrong' side of the hill on which it stands. There is a track leading across from Wincle village and paths down into the road-less tributary valley of the Shell Brook, but no main road is nearer than the Leek-Macclesfield route (A523) two miles distant and four hundred feet lower to the south-west. From Wincle Grange there is a clear view to Bosley Cloud, three miles away across the broadening Dane Valley to the south-west. This is the westernmost ridge of the south Pennines and presents a dramatic scarp face or 'nose' to the north, overlooking the plain near North Rode and Bosley villages. Up on the Cloud is the only true Neolithic chambered tomb not situated on carboniferous limestone; it is called 'the Bridestones'.

Downstream of the confluence of the Shell Brook with the Dane the valley suddenly widens and the river flows under the Leek–Macclesfield road at Hugbridge, the old boundary between Staffordshire and Cheshire, for the Dane has acted as such all the way down from Three Shire Heads. It is thought that the original bridge here took its name from the Norman Hugo de Mara, who held Bosley in 1080.

So the Dane winds on across the Cheshire Plain, leaving the brown uplands behind. The highest gritstone hills are conspicuous far out into the plain; the huge Post Office telecommunications tower on top of Sutton Common makes that height easy to identify, and the truncated cone of Shutlingsloe cannot be mistaken for any other feature. By way of an ending to this chapter I will recall a mysterious tale of these wild and unusual western hills.

The day I have in mind was a cool, grey one in early autumn. The morning hills were hazy with mist, but as we strode out from the isolated village of Flash the clouds began to part and a pale sun lit distant slopes where lonely farms seemed to wake and to lose their chilly, hostile countenances.

Soon we came to a smallholding at Knotbury. The bridle track passed below the house. In an open-fronted shed to one side was a fine little cart, its body painted blue, its wheels and shafts red. A hoop of metal curved above the body and to this were fastened masses of pink and white paper flowers, recently used, we deduced, at a local fête or gala.

No horse or pony was in evidence, or any human form, but a flock of hens were scratching about the bridle track and open-fronted sheds. They were birds as bright as the flower-decked cart and fussed over by the proudest of pouter-breasted bantam cocks, his erect comb shining vivid scarlet as he came between us and his busy dames.

Crouching low in the long, dying grass near the silent house were several cats – tabby, tortoiseshell and marmalade. They were wary of our passing but did not leave their temporary nests in the grass. The house gazed blandly at us: no sign of life within, but we were sure it was still a home, because the hens and the cats, and a dish-cloth swinging on the line, were evidence of continued human occupation.

Our route followed the bridle track, now rutted and stony, below the gritstone slope of Turn Edge. The track slanted down towards the River Dane, where it ran out of sight between trees and rocky banks. Between the point where we now looked down and the river were several tumble-walled fields and several farm buildings. Dark shapes littered the perimeter of one field.

The first building we came to was one of those typical multi-purpose structures; built of local gritstone it served as barn, loose-boxes for calves and a cowshed – or, more accurately, it had done so in the past, for now it seemed completely neglected. Old horseshoes and medicine bottles were pushed in some of the narrow ventilation slits of that portion serving as a barn. (What hidden treasure there must still be in deserted farm buildings up and down the country.)

The field below slopes steadily towards the side of the river, where sycamores were growing. Around its edge were parked a whole collection of old farm implements. It seemed as though a sale of the farmer's machinery had long ago been prepared but, for some reason, had never taken place. The seed-drill, flat-roller, dray and root-chopper were steadily rusting away, close beside the gritstone boundary walls.

Just below the field were more odd-shaped buildings (a pigsty, an open-fronted shed and a cart-shed), and hereabouts was the smell of death. The stench sizzled through the sharp upland air; we soon traced its source. Looking through the opening made for hay to be forked from cart to interior (a 'picking hole') of one shed, we could see the black and bloated form of an Aberdeen Angus heifer – dead these last seven days, we guessed. But why had not the body been removed? And were not there any more animals on this farm above the Dane?

In the little lean-to shed nearby we peered into the darkness and saw, as the vaguest shape at first, the hideous profile of a tent from which a white skull protruded. As our eyes became accustomed to the dim light within, we were able to recognize the tent as parchment-like hide sagging over a framework of bones, and the skull at one end was the head of a half-grown cow. How long this corpse had rested therein we could only guess at.

Now our curiosity was really aroused, and we went down to the sycamores beside the gurgling Dane. Poking through the trees some distance downstream were the chimney stacks of a house, and we went on down towards it. There were curtains to the windows and a broom stood by the front door. No smoke issued from the chimneys, and all the windows were shut. We knocked at the door but there was no answer.

Peering through a window, we could see the dimly-lit living-room. A dresser stood against the far wall, its shelves filled with old china and glass. An old wooden settle occupied the space below the window, and ashes still lay in the grate of the Yorkshire range. The other window revealed the tiny parlour where pot dogs gazed down from a high and shady mantelpiece. By standing back it was possible to see the brass bedsteads beside the bedroom windows, beds piled high with folded linen and coloured quilts. Clearly no one was resident here, though they could not have vacated the place long ago.

To the left of the house a low, stone building jutted at right angles, its back wall parallel with the River Dane. We opened the little door of the structure and peeped in; it was a wash-house and lavatory. There were two circular lavatory holes in the scrubbed wooden bench, and these opened directly over the river – truly a two-seater water closet!

An atmosphere of melancholy pervaded this part of the dale, an air of sadness tinged with mystery. We climbed up the steep and rutted track from the Dane to the hard lane at Knar Farm and on by Far Hole Edge and so came in half an hour to the farm at Burntcliff Top. By a roaring fire we talked to the rosy-cheeked farmwife as we drank her tea.

"It's a long and strange tale," she said. "The old folk have been taken away – but there's more to it than that. But it would be a brave person who told you more than what I've said." It was clear that that was all we were going to learn from her.

Soon we were walking along the pretty lane by Pearls and Midgley Gates to Allgreave. Then we had the glorious profile of Shutlingsloe ahead of us, truly Peakland's wonder hill.

The sheep were calling restlessly as we made our way towards the top by way of Higher Nabbs. The shepherd there had little information to offer. "Aye, it's a sorry tale, but the old man and his missus have gone away and that's that," he said;

then added as if he realized he had not really told us anything new. "The business is best left alone – I wouldn't venture down yonder, no, not for good money. Not now." Then he had turned and, calling to his dog, went off across a field of curly green kale.

We came upon an old mowing machine on the flanks of the hill, its cutter bar searching the sky like some old gibbet. The afternoon was well advanced and grey clouds were threatening as we reached the sharp, little top of Shutlingsloe. Yellow sunbeams shafted through the cloud layers on to the Cheshire Plain, miles away westwards. Black shapes twisted in the cold air above the valley, a dozen homing rooks with half-menacing calls.

Far away their croaking mingled with the baying of a pack of hounds. High on our windy hill we thought again of that secret in the empty dale and the folk who had once been there. For all we knew those rooks, now the slightest of black specks far out over the plain and lit now and then by sunbeams, could be the spirits of those vanished dales men who had left their corner of Peakland in such strange circumstances.

One thing was certain – the local inhabitants were not going to tell us the story, no matter how fascinating it might be. As we went down from Shutlingsloe in the fading light of that autumn afternoon, the hounds could still be heard under Whetstone Ridge where the River Dane is born; their unhappy calls seemed to epitomize the feelings of that day. We would probably never know the tale – only the forlorn farm, the dead animals and the crumbling implements where hedge sparrows and wrens build their nests.

21

The Rape of Sylva

Most of us have a favourite area which is considered as the ultimate haven, a place where we are most at home, a place usually
associated with childhood memory. In the mind it is held in
esteem as the promised land of protection where, in retrospect,
childhood dreams were made and where, upon return, dreams
of the past come close to reality.

Such an ultimate haven for me is the far-spreading country
occupied by Monk Wood, in the incomparable coal-measure
country of the north-east of Derbyshire. It stands at the central
point of a countryside which is truly 'home' and which has
remained largely unaltered through the passage of the years.

This extensive and largely natural woodland stands at the
heart of a remarkably broad tract of wild country. It is, for
instance, two and a half miles in a straight line from the environs of Sheepbridge westwards to Brindwoodgate. Likewise it
is almost as far from north to south between Dronfield Hill Top
and Cutthorpe Four Lane Ends. No public road used to cross
this beautiful wilderness, a haven for the flora and fauna which
are its heritage.

Though called 'Monk Wood', the woodland is correctly divi-
sible into several parts, each with a name of great antiquity.
Overlooking the lower Drone Valley above Unstone Green and
Sheepbridge are Loundes, Little Loundes and Brierley Woods.
To the west are Roecar, Roughpiece and Blackpiece Woods.
'Monk Wood' is correctly the western portion of the tract, and
beyond are the fringe districts occupied by Lees, Hollins
Spring, School, Grasscroft and Long Acre Woods. Almost all of
this area occupies land sloping towards the south, to the banks
of the Barlow Brook as it meanders eastwards to join the Drone
at Sheepbridge. One wood alone of this complex lies across the

Barlow Brook; the north-facing and highly conspicuous Cobnar Wood.

Throughout recorded history the district has been wooded and takes its name from medieval ecclesiastical associations. I am certain that the name is derived from a grant of land to a monastic foundation. It was probably a close association with Beauchief Abbey a few miles to the north (for it is known that there was a considerable traffic between this abbey and its penitentiary at Harewood Grange at the edge of Holy Moor to the west of Chesterfield) that gave this woodland its name. It is likely that such monastic journeyings would traverse this woodland, and there may well have been rights of wood-gathering and pig-grazing. According to S. P. Yeatman, the centrally situated Monkwood Farm was formerly 'the Mounks house' (*The Feudal History of the County of Derby, 1886–1907*), and in the Portland Collection is a record that in 1581 the building was called 'Monkwoddfeyld house'.

The great charm of the district lies in a combination of the gentle topography (though not so gentle as to be uninteresting) and the fine natural woodland. Today we can only guess at the excellent state of timber here a century ago, and in medieval times it must have been a limited reflection of Sherwood. Mention of that Nottinghamshire fastness reminds me that Monk Wood is firmly associated with Robin Hood. Robin Hood's Well, a short distance above the Middle Riding, is marked on the $2\frac{1}{2}$-inch OS map as a well, and from the never-ending flow a brook is born which has its own small hollow falling southwards to the main valley. This well is a place of pilgrimage, where we used to collect the abundant frog-spawn in spring and where ferns grow luxuriantly beneath the dark canopy of trees about the spring. Two of these trees are old hollies, and on them my parents carved their initials in the twenties. In childhood I, too, carved my initials, together with those of a friend – a real family tree. Those initials are as clear today as when they were created and represent something of a physical link with the past, with happy days spent in unconscious freedom in every season in the wild.

In the years immediately following 1900 considerable areas of central and western Monk Wood were replanted – the carved stones marking the lots can still be seen though much of the original and planted woodland was felled after World War II. This resulted in a drastic change in the countenance of the area and, at the time, seemed a tragedy. Since that time some areas have been replanted, notably Roughpiece and Blackpiece Woods on the flanks below Bull Close Farm. Other areas have grown up again into woodland by a process of natural regeneration. A large proportion of western Monk Wood has taken on the appearance of lovely, mature woodland in the last two decades. On examination much of this countenance, though, is composed of young and ill-formed tree growth. The silver birches dominate and present as beautiful a prospect to the eye as ever, but the young oaks and sycamores are not on the whole going to develop into fine specimens for a long period, for they are in need of thinning and brashing. Because they are self-set or have sprouted from felled bowls, they are wide-branched and bent, not the ideal forester's tree but typical of natural regeneration; they possess their own form of wild beauty.

It is true to say that many parts of this woodland have reached again the status of true forest, albeit immature and punctuated by a very few ancient specimen trees which have miraculously escaped the woodman's axe.

In modern jargon Monk Wood was the traditional 'lung' for Dronfield people. Here they came on summer evenings and Sunday afternoons for relaxation and exercise, and for blackberries in September and firewood during the winter. The place used to resound to the laughter and chattering of children and parents; today it is virtually silent. It seems that with the universal acquisition of the motor car tastes have become more sophisticated, and the majority, in their hopeless search for ease and a far-flung place in the sun, have overlooked the fact that the simplest pleasures are almost always the best – that and the fact of lives packed ever more tightly by materialism has brought peace and solitude to this wonderland just over the hill and above a certain golden valley. Into this very woodland my grandparents would wander, to gaze afar from beside the Pig Gate at the edge of the golf links, far towards the western moorland horizon which still fringes this view. Here came my parents in summers long ago, and my earliest memories are of these very glades under bright sunlight – how my pram took a pounding up and down that rutted sandstone track to the

Middle Riding. Then during the latter felling operations Aunt Mary took me with her friends the Websters on early morning 'chipping' expeditions. I used to wonder why chips were available in the great, uninhabited wood, and it was a long time before it became clear to me that the small pieces of wood and bark left by the woodmen which we collected by the sackful and transported back down Hallowes Lane on a cratch were those very chips! Later parties of Dronfield and Unstone people went to the woods with sacks, buckets and prams to cart off loads of coal exposed by the opencast working that followed felling operations in eastern Monk Wood; but I never had an opportunity to help in this later harvest.

A later memory comes to mind – of a rusting lorry we came across far along the Top Riding, somewhere below Blackpiece Wood. It had been left by the woodmen, and I had hopes of getting it mobile, but that particular dream never materialized and it was at last dragged off or broken up. Anyway, the downward view from the site of that lorry is well loved, in particular for the glimpse of Monkwood Farm. Here the Millington family lived for a long period and served teas under the ancient fruit trees in the orchard – the leaning pear tree where we used to swing still stands – and now the well-known Walker family occupy this, the only dwelling truly within the confines of the present wood.

From the 'cross-roads' a short distance to the north of Monkwood Farm there was a spectacular view towards Sheepbridge Works. It was a photograph of this very vista taken by the late Philip Jones of Dronfield which won Second Prize in a worldwide competition open to the best of the world's photographers. Though his life was a constant battle against ill health, Philip Jones was able to produce works of great beauty, and in this particular creation he showed the amalgamation of industry with nature, distant smoke and chimneys framed by nearer vegetation and crowned by the glory of great cloud formations. I purposely used the past tense with regard to this eastward view, for most of the arresting industrial skyline down the valley has gone, and the nearer trees have been replaced by open fields which reach right up to this 'cross-roads'. Away across those fields lie the small reservoirs fed by the Barlow Brook and constructed by the Sheepbridge Coal and Iron Company to supply the works with cooling water.

In recent years Broombank Road has been extended up the broad valley floor westwards from Sheepbridge. Beside it has grown up a new industrial estate – grey and brown smoke, dust, the groan of machinery and the alarmingly drab uniformity of warehouses and workshops. It cannot be so very long ere those little reservoirs lie alongside the perimeter of an ugly factory fence.

It is now forty years since a by-pass road was suggested to take through traffic using the A61 (Leeds-Exeter) trunk road between Sheffield and Chesterfield. The plans were to build a fast highway to avoid Unstone and Dronfield which would swing around to the west of these valley settlements. It was a threat to the fastness of Monk Wood, that remaining jewel of wild country so close to this well-populated district. The outbreak of World War Two and subsequent economic difficulties meant the shelving of the plan; the threat went into the back of interested minds – Monk Wood remained a haven.

How singularly inappropriate it was that in 1970 – European Conservation Year – the Ministry of Transport decided to implement their scheme for wholesale destruction of some of the finest and least adulterated countryside in this part of England. This action highlighted the arrogance of some Government and local government departments who formulate their wonderful plans from an office desk with, it seems, complete disregard for the land over which, unfortunately, they hold control.

When the diabolical plans for the Unstone and Dronfield By-Pass were revised, a very sensible scheme was presented whereby the by-pass would be re-routed to the east of the existing A61, sweeping by way of districts already to some extent spoilt by industrialization – close to the confines of the Rother Valley, from Whittington and so into south-eastern Sheffield. The Ministry of Transport decided in favour of the western route. One saving grace for which we must forever be grateful is that, due to objections, the original route (by way of Dunston Hole, Cobnar Wood-top, Lee Bridge, the Galloping Close, School Wood and so across the already desecrated Gosforth Valley west of Dronfield) was modified to pass instead through the heart of Monk Wood and across the axis of the famous Brimington Anticline to the west of Dronfield Hill Top.

It could have been argued at the time that a new road with a minimum width of seventy feet was not going to interfere unduly with this unspoilt country. However, during construction much more than the final width of the road was upset and remains as cutting sides or embankment slopes.

Though it is possible to wander in the remaining woodland out of sight of fast-moving traffic, the whole ecosystem of the area has been affected. There is an almost constant noise from traffic, and serious pollution inevitably results from exhaust gases and, in winter, from the run-off of surface drainage having a high salt content. One simply has to look at the sorry state of many of the trees and hedgerows bordering the old A61 road and compare them with similar specimens where such pollution does not exist at present to understand the long-term effect of the By-Pass on Monk Wood.

Those who considered the preservation of this particular wilderness were given until the middle of August 1970 to complain to the Minister of Transport. My objection consisted of a general one of destruction of the environment and a special plea for the avoidance of the historic Robin Hood's Well, close beside the Middle Riding not far from Monk Wood Farm. It may be of some interest to mention a few points from the letter of reply from the Midland Road Construction Unit, Leamington Spa, in November 1970.

"There was, as you suggest in your letter, an earlier proposal that the By-Pass should go to the east of Dronfield. This was the main alternative considered prior to the making of the line Order in 1963 but apart from being much more expensive, the eastern route would have had far more serious effects on residential property."

Concerning landscaping the reply explained that there would be "tree planting on the banks, verges and central reservation". What we see today is largely grass-covered slope; I cannot see the trees on the margins of the By-Pass or on the central reservation. Maybe the idea was to wait for Nature to do the job at no expense – except for the many initial years of waiting and emptiness!

With relief I noted that "Robin Hood's Well will not be

affected in any way by the road work. It will be some 120 feet away from the nearest point of the By-Pass." What was not mentioned, of course, was the fact that the huge curl of concrete forming the southern end of the bridle bridge over the new road would rise close to this remarkable spring and its sheltering hollies, dominating the scene and destroying most of the sylvan charm of this secret arbour.

In early summer the western district in particular has an astonishing carpet of blue, as it has every May these last thousand years, and crab apple blossom contrasts brilliantly with the freshly burst silver birches. There is dark green and happy resignation in the height of summer, and in autumn the land is a treasure-house burnished and flashing. When the snow lies thickly frosted on every branch, it seems indeed a sacrilege to tread this new and secret land. I remember writing in 1971 that "it may not be long ere all we have of the former glory is memory."

During the autumn of 1973 work began on the By-Pass, and the biggest single undertaking was the excavation of a cutting through the ridge extending westwards from the edge of Hallowes golf course towards Lees Common. The idea was to create a one-hundred-feet-deep cutting – the Monk Wood Cut – to reduce the gradient on the new road and to baffle traffic noise and visual impact on the woodland (the last, I am sure, a very secondary consideration in the plans). This was the deepest cutting on any new road in Britain, and some idea can be obtained of the scale of the thing when it is realized that the easily excavated mudstones here were removed at the rate of more than seventy-thousand cubic metres per week in mid December 1973. The cutting was created between September 1973 and July 1974 and in all 735,200 cubic metres of material were removed, including six hundred tonnes of coal in the previously worked Blackshale seam which was delivered to NCB screening plants.

This large cutting was created only with the overcoming of several problems, the most serious being sliding wedge failure which would result in large areas of the sandstone and mudstone strata sliding down and blocking the road in the cutting. Dr D. S. Buist has written in some detail of the measures taken by the Midland Road Construction Unit to prevent this happening. At the western face of the cutting, with the strata dipping steeply away, there was no threat of sliding, and the slopes are as much as one to one, though less competent silt-stones and mudstones were cut less steeply – one to one and a half and one to three respectively. On the eastern side of the cut-ting, though, the gently dipping strata was exposed and could easily slide down the slope – sliding wedge failure in action. To prevent this, it was originally thought that rock bolting to 'pin' the sandstone and mudstone layers together would be a feasible solution, but later appraisal caused other methods to be used. These included the provision of some herring-bone drains on the weak, eastern side of the cutting and by overdigging by about two feet where the massive sandstones and mudstones occurred and replacing them with recompacted sandstone. In order to give something of a 'landscape' effect, an attempt was made to leave some exposed rock features – to a height of about four feet as a safe maximum, though it is generally agreed that such small-scale exposure on such an extensive cutting face appears insignificant and that rocks at least six feet deep are necessary to create any satisfactory effect.

The route of the new By-Pass encountered many old iron-stone and coal workings. Some of those discovered dated from before 1872, the date when it became a statutory requirement to keep accurate records of mining activities. Bell-pits, shafts and adits were uncovered in the Monk Wood Cut, particu-larly near the site of Grasscroft Colliery at the northern end of the cutting. The Silkstone seam of productive coal-measures was excavated to a depth of a yard below its formation level, then sealed with concrete.

At last all the activity came to an end, and the By-Pass was opened to traffic in 1975. As a friend observed at the time, no one using that sweep of bare tarmac is going to notice more than a pretty view – they will certainly not see the fairies be-neath the trees. No, the magic of those several woods has re-ceded, bisected by noise and speed and fumes. One must now go to the still and quiet corners to find the magic which once covered all this country like a huge, green blanket.

Where the Barlow Brook trickles under Lee Bridge and the old bridle road goes between Great Barlow and Dronfield, several paths lead to that soft, green land, into the slanting groves of Broombank and the flat-topped, bracken-clad height above the site of Broombank Colliery. One can wander between the graceful shafts of silver birches, under the rowans, and look far across the vale to a hundred brown-roofed farmsteads and dotted slopes this side of the moors. In certain conditions – a sodden June evening or a perfectly still and balmy September afternoon – no sound comes across the wood, no suggestion of the dirty, ugly new road.

Drawing nearer to that By-Pass, walking up to the northeast, I am reminded of John Clare's lament for the simple pleasures of years long passed as the groan of traffic reaches one's ears:

> Summer's pleasures they are gone like visions every one,
> And the cloudy days of autumn and of winter cometh on.
> I tried to call them back, but unbidden they are gone
> Far away from heart and eye and for ever far away.
> Dear heart, and can it be that such raptures meet decay?

Yes, can it indeed be that such glorious raptures, such magic memories, those dusky pathways between the bracken which has grown unhindered a thousand years, and the peace only momentarily uninterrupted by a jay's laughter or a wood pigeon's clattering wingbeats, come to an end here forever? No, the time must come when that tarmac sweep will crack and silver birches will root there and Clare's wishful thinking will be realized:

> Where silence sitteth now on the wild heath as her own
> Like a ruin of the past all alone.

Until that time I can wander on the Broombank slopes or in Blackpiece Wood or over the ridge in Brierley Wood, and quite easily believe the place is unchanged –

> I never get between the trees
> But I smell the Highgate air;
> Nor I never come on a woodland ride
> But my home is there,
> And along the sky the Pennine's edge
> Far and high and bare.

Index